LONGMAN PRA

INSOLVENCY LAW

2nd EDITION

Steven A Frieze
Solicitor and Licensed Insolvency Practitioner,
Partner in Brooke North & Goodwin
Leeds and Gibraltar

SERIES EDITOR
CM Brand, Solicitor and Lecturer in Law
University of Liverpool

© Longman Group UK Ltd 1993

ISBN 0 85121 0805

Published by
Longman Law, Tax and Finance
Longman Group UK Ltd
21–27 Lamb's Conduit Street, London WC1N 3NJ

Associated offices
Australia, Hong Kong, Malaysia, Singapore, USA

A CIP catalogue record for this book is available from the British Library.

Printed and bound in Great Britain by
Biddles Ltd, Guildford and King's Lynn

CONTENTS

11 Administrations

CHAPTER 1

DEFINITIONS

1.1 Source material

Statutes	The Insolvency Act 1986
	Deeds of Arrangement Act 1914
Statutory Instruments	The Insolvency Rules 1986 (SI No 1925) as amended
	The Insolvent Partnerships Order 1986 (SI No 2142)
	Administration of Insolvent Estates of Deceased Persons Order 1986 (SI No 1999)
	Insolvency Practitioner Regulations 1986 (SI No 1995)
	Insolvency Proceedings (Monetary Limits) Order 1986 (SI No 1996)
	Insolvency Fees Order 1986 (SI No 2030)
	Cooperation of Insolvency Court (Designation of Relevant Countries and Territories Order) 1986 (SI No 2123)

1.2 Definitions

The Act

The Insolvency Act 1986—which came into force on 29 December 1986 and applies to all insolvencies (except deeds of assignment) commenced (by petition or otherwise) after that date. The parts of the Act relating to companies applies not only to England and Wales but also to Scotland. All insolvencies commenced before 29 December 1986 continue to be subject to the Bankruptcy Act 1914 or the Companies Act 1985 as the case may be, except that there are in Sched 11 to the Act certain transitional provisions including:

- power for the Secretary of State to appoint trustees or liquidators to old Act cases;
- automatic discharge from bankruptcy of all old Act bankrupts on 29 December 1989;

- power for the trustee or liquidator to agree costs (instead of taxation) (r 7.34(6)).

Administrator	The person appointed by the court to handle the affairs of a company the subject of an administration order.
Administrative receiver	The person appointed by the holder of a floating charge debenture over a company's assets to collect in and realise the assets of that company to repay the indebtedness to the debenture holder.
Authorised (or licensed) insolvency practitioner	The person (usually an accountant or solicitor) authorised by the Department of Trade and Industry (DTI) or a professional body to act as trustee, nominee, supervisor, liquidator, administrative receiver or administrator. Only such a person can hold any of these offices.
Bankrupt	See **undischarged bankrupt**.
Bankruptcy order	The court order making an individual bankrupt (this replaces the concept of the receiving order and adjudication of bankruptcy in the old Act cases).
Compulsory liquidation	The placing of the company into liquidation as a result of an application to the court, usually by a creditor (see chapter 7).
Contributory	Shareholder.
CVA	Company voluntary arrangement (see chapter 11).
DTI	Department of trade and industry (headed up by the Secretary of State).
Fee	The court fee payable as prescribed by the Supreme Court Fees Order or the County Court Fees Order.
Insolvent	The state of not being able to pay one's debts as they fall due *or* having an excess of liabilities over assets.
IVA	Individual voluntary arrangement (see chapter 4).

Licensed authorised practitioner	See **authorised insolvency practitioner**.
Liquidation	See winding up.
Liquidator	The person appointed to deal with the assets and liabilities of the company or partnership once the resolution to wind up has been passed or a compulsory winding up order has been made.
Member	Shareholder.
Nominee	The person chosen by the individual or corporate debtor to report on the debtor's proposals for an IVA or CVA.
Official Receiver	The civil servant employed by the DTI to head the regional offices whose responsibilities cover bankruptcies and compulsory liquidations.
Proof of debt	The document submitted in an insolvency to establish a creditor's claim. It may be informal (by eg letter) or in a prescribed form (in bankruptcy and compulsory liquidation).
Provisional liquidator	The person appointed by the court to deal with the affairs of the company until a compulsory winding up order.
Proxy	The authority given by a creditor or member to another person to attend and vote at a meeting on behalf of the creditor or member.
Receiver	The person appointed by the court for some specific purpose or the person appointed by a mortgagee to exercise his rights over the charged property under the Law of Property Act 1925 (not to be confused with the Official Receiver or administrative receiver).
The Rules	The Insolvency Rules 1986 (as amended)—these Rules apply where the Act applies. Where the old Acts continue to apply so do the Bankruptcy Rules 1952 and the Companies (Winding Up) Rules 1949. There are separate rules dealing with insolvent partnerships,

3

	insolvent deceased's estates and deeds of arrangement.
Supervisor	The person appointed to supervise the implementation of the debtor's proposals for an IVA or CVA once approved by creditors (and members).
Trustee	Either

- in bankruptcy—the authorised insolvency practitioner appointed to deal with the estate of the bankrupt;

or

- under a deed of arrangement—the authorised insolvency practitioner appointed to deal with the estate of the person who entered into the deed.

Undischarged bankrupt

Someone against whom a bankruptcy order has been made and who has not been discharged from bankruptcy.

Voluntary liquidation

The placing of the company into liquidation by resolution of the members—there are two types of voluntary liquidation

- members' voluntary liquidation; and
- creditors' voluntary liquidation.

The first of these does not involve insolvency and comes about merely because the (shareholders) members wish to have the value of their shareholding realised eg on the retirement of the principals of the company or when the purpose for which the company was incorporated has been fulfilled. Creditors' voluntary liquidations are dealt with in chapter 8.

Winding-up

(Or liquidation)—the procedure whereby the assets of a company (or partnership) are gathered in and realised, the liabilities met and the surplus, if any, distributed to members.

CHAPTER 2

BANKRUPTCY

2.1 Introduction

To make an individual bankrupt, it is necessary to have grounds and to choose the right court to which to make application to petition. The choice of court is set out below. A statutory demand is often prepared and served as non-compliance with such a demand is one of the grounds for petitioning for bankruptcy (see section 2.3 below). The procedure for creditor's petition is set out in section 2.4 and a debtor's own petition in section 2.5. Subsequent sections deal with the procedure then to be followed to ensure that the debtor is made bankrupt, that a trustee is appointed and that the debtor's estate is properly administrated.

2.2 Which court has jurisdiction?

2.2.1 The High Court alone has jurisdiction in bankruptcy proceedings if (r 6.9(1)):

- the debtor has resided or carried on business within the London insolvency district for the greater part of the last six months or for a longer period than in any other insolvency district; or
- he is not resident in England or Wales; or
- his residence or place of business is unknown to the petitioner; or
- the petition is presented by a government department based on an unsatisfied execution or a statutory demand in which it was stated that if a bankruptcy petition was necessary, it would be presented in the High Court.

2.2.2 The county court has jurisdiction in all other cases. A bankruptcy petition must be presented in the county court for the insolvency district in which the debtor has resided or carried on business for the longest period in the last six months (r 6.9(2)). If the debtor has carried on business in one area and resided in another, the place where he carried on business determines the choice of court (r 6.9(3)). If the debtor has carried on business in more than one area, then the place where he had his principal place of business or had his principal place of business for the longest period determines the choice of court (r 6.9(4)). If the debtor is already the subject of an individual voluntary arrangement (IVA), then the court dealing with the IVA must also deal with the bankruptcy. All petitions must contain sufficient information to establish the correctness of the choice of court (r 6.9(5)).

2.2.3 The London Insolvency District comprises the City of London and the districts of the following county courts:

Barnet	Mayor and City of London
Bow	Marylebone
Brentford	Shoreditch
Central London	Wandsworth
Clerkenwell	West London
Edmonton	Willesden
Lambeth	

2.2.4 No jurisdiction Not all county courts have bankruptcy jurisdiction. For a list of all the county courts in England and Wales showing which of those courts exercise bankruptcy jurisdiction see Appendix 1.

2.2.5 The wrong court If a petition is presented in the wrong court, the court can: transfer proceedings to the correct court; allow the proceedings to continue where they are, provided that that court has bankruptcy jurisdiction; or strike out the proceedings. (r 7.12).

2.2.6 Transfer between courts Proceedings can be transferred from the High Court to a county court or vice versa at any time (r 7.11). The court can transfer proceedings of its own motion or on the application of an interested party (Official Receiver, trustee, creditor or the debtor) (r 7.13).

2.3 The statutory demand

2.3.1 What is a statutory demand? A statutory demand is a document prepared by a creditor in the prescribed form requiring the debtor to pay the debt referred to in the demand or to secure or compound (that means provide security for the debt or come to some arrangement for the payment of the debt with the creditor) that debt to the satisfaction of the creditor within three weeks after the demand has been served.

2.3.2 Why is a demand necessary? To found a petition for the bankruptcy of the debtor, a creditor must show that the debtor owes a debt above the minimum level (currently £750) as prescribed by the Insolvency Proceedings (Monetary Limits) Order 1986 (SI No 1196) and the debtor appears to be unable to pay that debt or appears to have no reasonable prospect of being able to pay that debt (s 267). A debtor appears to be unable to pay a debt if he has been served with a statutory demand and more than three weeks have elapsed since the demand was served upon him and he has not complied with the demand nor applied to have it set aside (s 268). In the alternative, a petition can be based on an unsatisfied execution and a debt above the minimum level.

2.3.3 Form There are three forms of statutory demand set out in Sched 4 to the Rules:

- Form 6.1—demand for a debt presently due but not based on a judgment;
- Form 6.2—demand for a debt presently due based on a judgment or order of the court;
- Form 6.3—demand for a debt due at a future time.

2.3.4 Completion The full name of the debtor should be given but if it is not known, it is sufficient to say even 'SMITH (MALE)'. The full name and address of the creditor should be stated; only one debt can be included as the debt. The amount of the debt must be stated and the consideration for it, as must details of the judgment or order, if any. If interest is being claimed, this should be shown separately and the rate charged shown and why it is being claimed. If a statutory demand is served by a Crown department and it intends to present a petition in the High Court rather than in the county court, this must be stated in the demand. A statutory demand can only be made for an unsecured debt and if the creditor holds any security he must specify what it is and put a value on it so that the amount of the unsecured portion of his debt can be identified. The demand must be signed by the creditor himself or by someone authorised on his behalf, such as his solicitor. If the creditor is represented by a firm of solicitors, the demand must be signed by an individual solicitor of that firm in his own name with the name, address, reference and telephone number of the firm added afterwards. It is not correct for the demand to be signed in the firm's name.

On page 2 of the demand, the court to which the debtor can apply to have the demand set aside must be given. This court will be either the High Court (if the debtor resides or carries on business in the area of the London Insolvency District) or one of the county courts specified in Appendix 1.

The prescribed period for compliance with the demand is 21 days but if the demand has been served abroad, different time limits apply and must be inserted in the demand in accordance with the Extra Jurisdiction Tables to be found in the *Supreme Court Practice (Practice Note (Bankruptcy: Service Abroad)* [1988] 1 WLR 461).

If the debt is payable at a future time, Form 6.3 must be used instead of either Forms 6.1 and 6.2 and the creditor must state why he believes the debtor has no reasonable prospect of paying the debt when it falls due.

2.3.5 Service The creditor must do all that is reasonable to bring the demand to the debtor's attention and, if practicable in the circumstances, personally serve the demand (r 6.3(2)). If personal service is not possible, postal service, insertion through a letter box or substituted service is permitted. (*Practice Note (Bankruptcy: Substituted Service)* [1987] 1 WLR 82.) It is up to the creditor to satisfy the court, when presenting a petition based upon failure to comply with a statutory demand served other than personally, that he has done all that is necessary. As there is no application to the court for leave to use substituted service, the creditor will have to satisfy the court ex post facto that the use of substituted service was justified. If the postal service is used, the demand is deemed served on the seventh day after posting if first class post is used. If service by advertisement is used (this can only apply if the creditor has obtained a judgment against the debtor), time runs from the date of the first advertisement. Leave to serve out of the jurisdiction is not required but different time limits for compliance apply, see above.

An affidavit of service of the demand is required. There are prescribed forms of affidavit:

- Form 6.11—where personal service is effected;
- Form 6.12—where substituted service is used.

Form 6.11 is the more commonly required. The affidavit of service must exhibit the demand, any acknowledgement in writing from the debtor and a copy of the newspaper advertisement (where applicable).

2.3.6 Time for compliance   The debtor is deemed to be unable to pay his debts if at least three weeks have elapsed since a demand was served on him and he has not complied with it. The day the demand was served and the day the petition was presented are ignored for the purpose of calculating if the correct time has been allowed. Similar rules apply for calculating the period of 18 days within which the debtor must apply to the court for the demand to be set aside if he so wishes. Service after 4 pm on a business day or service on a weekend or bank holiday is deemed to have taken place on the next business day. If the creditor can show that there is a serious possibility of the debtor's property being diminished in value in the three-week period after service of a demand, a petition can be presented sooner (though not until after the statutory demand has been served) but a bankruptcy order cannot be made until after the three-week period has elapsed (s 271).

2.3.7 Defects in the demand   Rule 7.55, which permits a court to waive an irregularity or defect in insolvency proceedings, does not apply to statutory demands.

Where the wrong form has been used (eg Form 6.1 instead of Form 6.2), the demand will not be set aside if the debtor was not prejudiced (*In Re a Debtor (No 1 of 1987)* [1989] 2 All ER 46). If the demand has overstated the amount due or if the debtor disputes part of the debt, provided there remains a debt exceeding £750 which is not disputed, then the demand will not be set aside (*In Re a Debtor (No 490 SD 1991)* (*The Times*, 9 April (1992)) overruling *In Re a Debtor (No 10 of 1988)* [1989] 1 WLR 406). For the procedure as to setting aside a statutory demand, see below.

2.3.8 Setting aside The application to set aside a demand must be made within 18 days after service of the demand. The court has power to extend the time for applying and will usually grant leave for a late application if any reason for the delay is given. The application for an extension of time is made to the High Court or circuit judge (not the registrar or district judge). The fee payable is £15.

An affidavit in support of an application is required to set aside a demand stating when the demand was received and the grounds of the application. A copy of the demand must be exhibited. Four copies of the application and the affidavit must be lodged at court together with the fee of £10. The application is heard by the registrar or district judge. Examples of the reasons for asking for a demand to be set aside are:

- the debt is disputed in whole or part (and there is not at least £750 admitted);
- the debt is not payable now;
- the debtor is prepared to secure or compound for the debt to the creditor's satisfaction in a stated way;
- the debt is secured;
- the debtor has a counterclaim or set-off equal to or exceeding the claim;
- execution of the judgment has been stayed;
- the demand does not comply with the rules.

The application must be made in the appropriate court. To ascertain which is the appropriate court, see 2.2 above. The application automatically causes the time for compliance with the demand to cease to run (r 6.4(3)). If the registrar or district judge reading the papers ex parte is satisfied that the application is without merit, he may dismiss it without a hearing or notice to the creditor. If he is satisfied that the application has some merit, a hearing date will be fixed and notice will be given to the creditor or his solicitor.

At the hearing, if the court is satisfied that one of the matters referred to above applies, the demand will be set aside and the creditor is liable to have the costs of the application awarded against him. If the demand is not set aside, the court may make an order authorising the creditor to present a bankruptcy petition at a specified time (r 6.5(6)).

2.4 Creditors' petitions

2.4.1 Conditions for petitioning There are three conditions which must be satisfied for a bankruptcy petition to be presented to the court:

- the debtor must be domiciled or personally resident or carrying on business in England and Wales on the day on which the petition is presented or at any time in the previous three years (s 265(1));
- the debt owed by the debtor (or the total of the debts owing to the petitioners if there are two or more of them) must be above the minimum

level of £750 and be a liquidated sum payable immediately or at some certain future time (s 268); and

- the debtor must be unable to pay the debt or have no reasonable prospect of being able to pay. This requirement is satisfied if the debtor has been served with a statutory demand and has failed to comply with it nor had it set aside or an execution or other process issued against him in respect of that debt has been returned unsatisfied in whole or in part (s 268(1)).

2.4.2 Form
There are four prescribed forms of petition set out in the Rules:

- Form 6.7—on failure to comply with a statutory demand, debt payable immediately;
- Form 6.8—on failure to comply with a statutory demand, debt payable at a future date;
- Form 6.9—where execution returned unsatisfied;
- Form 6.10—on default in connection with IVA.

2.4.3 Completion
If two or more creditors jointly petition, all their details must be given. Anyone who can sue the debtor for the debt is classed as a creditor of the debtor for the purposes of the petition. Secured creditors must value their security and can only petition for the unsecured part of their debt or risk forfeiting their security.

The following information relating to the debtor must be given:

- his name, address, place of residence and occupation;
- the names in which he carried on business, if other than his true name and if alone or with others;
- the nature and address of his business;
- any previous names used by the debtor at the time the debt was incurred;
- his residential or business address at the time the debt was incurred (r 6.7(1)).

If the creditor knows that the debtor has used any other name, this must be stated in the petition (r 6.7(3)).

The petition must state:

- the amount, the consideration for it and the fact that it is still owing;
- when the debt was incurred or became due;
- if interest is included, how it has been calculated and the grounds for claiming it;
- that the debt is for a liquidated sum payable immediately and the debtor is unable to pay it or that the debt is payable at a certain future time and the debtor appears to have no reasonable prospect of being able to pay and, in either case, that the debt is unsecured.

If the petition is based upon a statutory demand, only the debt claimed in the demand can be included and interest accrued since the demand was served cannot be included (*Practice Directions* [1987] 1 WLR 81 and [1987] 1 WLR 1424). If the petition is based upon an unsatisfied execution, full particulars of the issuing court and the sheriff's or bailiff's return must be given (r 6.8(3)). The petition does not require dating, signing or witnessing.

If the petition is based on non-compliance with a statutory demand, care must be taken to recite correctly the details of service and in particular whether service was effected before or after 4 pm on business days or before or after 12 noon on Saturdays. It is no longer necessary to search to see if monies have been paid into the county court in satisfaction of any judgment debt obtained in that court.

It is still desirable to search for prior bankruptcy petitions even though there is no requirement to do so. The court tends to carry out such a search itself, but effort and cost can be saved by ascertaining before a further petition is issued that there is already one pending.

2.4.4 Verification A bankruptcy petition must be verified by an affidavit (r 6.12(1)). If the petition is based on failure to comply with a statutory demand and more than four months have elapsed since the demand was served, the reasons for the delay must be given in the affidavit. If no adequate explanation is given, the petition may be dismissed under s 266(3) but the court cannot refuse to allow the petition to be issued. The affidavit verifying the petition must exhibit a copy of the petition (r 6.12(3)). Form 6.13 in Sched 4 to the Rules is the prescribed form of affidavit verifying the petition.

2.4.5 Issue As to which court the petition must be presented in, see 2.2 above.

On issue the following are required:

- the petition together with two copies (and a further copy if voluntary arrangement is in force);
- if the petition is based upon failure to comply with a statutory demand, the affidavit of service of the demand;
- an affidavit verifying the petition;
- a receipt for the deposit payable to the Official Receiver (which the court will accept on behalf of the Official Receiver)—currently £270;
- the fee—currently £50.

All copies of the petition are sealed by the court and, save for one, handed back to the petitioner. The petition is endorsed by the court with details of the time, date and place of the hearing.

2.4.6 Service A sealed copy of the petition must be served personally on the debtor by a court bailiff, the petitioning creditor or his solicitor or someone instructed on their behalf. If service is effected after 4 pm on a business day or after 12 noon on a Saturday, service is deemed to have been effected on the next business day (RSC Ord 65 r 7). If a voluntary arrangement is in force, the supervisor must be served as well as the debtor unless it is the supervisor who is petitioning. If the court is satisfied that the debtor is keeping out of the way to avoid service of the petition, it may order substituted service (r 6.14(2)) and see also *Practice Note (Bankruptcy: Substituted Service)* [1987] 1 WLR 82.

An affidavit of service of the petition is required which must exhibit a sealed copy of the petition and, when substituted service has been ordered, a copy of that order. The affidavit of service must be filed in court immediately after service (r 6.15(2)). The form of affidavit of service is Form 6.17 in Sched 4. If substituted service has been utilised, Form 6.18 is required.

2.4.7 Consolidation of petitions Where two or more petitions have been presented against the same debtor, the court can order the consolidation of the proceedings on such terms as it thinks fit (r 6.236).

2.4.8 Hearing of the petition The petition cannot be heard until at least 14 days have elapsed since it was served unless the court is satisfied that an expedited hearing is warranted, the debtor is about to abscond or the debtor consents to an early hearing. If the debtor wishes to oppose the petition he must give notice to the petitioning creditor and file at court a notice specifying the grounds of his objection. A petition may be amended at any time with leave of the court.

Any creditor who intends to appear on the hearing of the petition must give notice to the petitioning creditor. The notice must state the amount of his debt and whether he intends to support or oppose the petition. The notice is Form 6.20 in Sched 4. The petitioning creditor must prepare a list of the creditors, if any, who have given notice of intention to appear or state on such a list that there are no creditors who have given notice of intention to appear. The list is prescribed Form 6.21. The list is handed to the court clerk before the commencement of the hearing. If the petitioning creditor fails to appear on the hearing, the petition may be dismissed and no further petitions against the same debtor would be allowed, without leave of the court (r 6.26). It is not necessary for the petitioning creditor himself to appear at the hearing if he is represented by solicitors.

The courts are unwilling to adjourn a petition more than once since it must not be allowed to hang over the debtor's head indefinitely. If, however, insufficient time has elapsed since the debtor was served with the petition, the hearing must be adjourned. If there is an adjournment, the petitioning creditor must inform all those creditors who have given notice of intention to appear and also inform the debtor. The order adjourning the petition (Form 6.23) is prepared by the court and the notice of adjournment (Form 6.24) is prepared by the petitioning creditor.

2.4.9 Substitution If the petitioning creditor has been paid his debt, the court may order that another creditor be substituted as petitioning creditor provided that creditor has given notice of his intention to appear on the hearing and wishes to prosecute the petition. The substituting creditor must also be owed a debt equal to the bankruptcy level, currently £750, and to have been in a position to present his own petition at the time the original petition was issued. If substitution is ordered the petition will need amendment and it will also have to be reserved. The hearing will have to be adjourned to a future date. Rules 6.30 and 6.31 deal with substitution. The order for substitution of a petitioner is Form 6.24A in Sched 4 to the Rules.

As an alternative to seeking substitution as petitioning creditor, if a creditor has given notice of his intention to appear on the hearing he may apply to the court for an order giving him control of the proceedings ('carriage of the petition') in place of the petitioning creditor. The court may make such an order if satisfied that the petitioning creditor does not intend to prosecute the petition either diligently or at all (r 6.31(2)). The court must not make such an order if satisfied that the petitioning creditor does not wish to pursue the petititon because he has been paid by a third party or by disposition of the debtor's own property with the approval of the court (r 6.32(3)). The change of carriage order is Form 6.24B. To obtain a change of carriage order the 'new' petitioner does not need to have been in a position to petition at the time when the petition was originally presented nor does he have to be owed more than the minimum debt of £750.

2.4.10 Dismissal and withdrawal A petition cannot be withdrawn except at the hearing and the court will dismiss a petition or give leave for it to be withdrawn only if the petitioning creditor files at court an affidavit setting out why he wants the petition dismissed or withdrawn. The affidavit must include details of any payments made by the debtor or arrangements for the securing or compounding of the debt together with details of where the monies came from that were used to pay or secure or compound the debt. On an application for leave to withdraw the petition or for dismissal of the petition, it is the practice of the court to adjourn the petition to a new hearing date so as to enable any other creditor to make an application to be substituted as petitioning creditor. The form of dismissal of a petition is Form 6.22.

2.4.11 Certificate of debt On the hearing of the petition, the petitioning creditor must satisfy the court that the debt is still owing. A certificate in the following form, signed by the person representing the petitioning creditor will suffice:

I certify that I have (my firm has) made enquiries of the petitioning creditor within the last business day prior to the hearing/adjourned hearing and to the best of my knowledge and belief the debt on which the petition is founded is still due and owing and has not been paid or secured or compounded for (save as to . . .).

Signed   . . . .
Dated   . . . .

A fresh certificate is required on each adjourned hearing.

2.4.12 The hearing For a bankruptcy order to be made, the court must be satisfied that the debt in respect of which the petition was presented has neither been paid (nor secured nor compounded for) or, if the debt is due at a future time, the debtor has no reasonable prospect of being able to pay when it falls due (s 271(1)). The court will not make a bankruptcy order and will dismiss the petition if it is satisfied that the debtor is able to pay all his debts or is satisfied that the debtor has made an offer to secure or compound for the debt and that that offer has been unreasonably refused. In determining whether the debtor is able to pay all his debts, his contingent and prospective liabilities must also be taken into account (s 271(3)).

If the court is satisfied that the statements in the petition are true and the debt on which it is founded has not been paid or secured or compounded for, then it *may* make a bankruptcy order (r 6.25(1))—note that the rule gives the court a discretion. Normally, where the petition is not opposed or is opposed only by 'connected' creditors, the petitioner can expect to succeed in his request for a bankruptcy order. If the petition is brought in respect of a judgment debt and there is an appeal pending against that judgment or execution on that judgment has been stayed, the court *may* stay or dismiss the petition (r 6.25(2)). If the court considers the appeal to be frivolous then it may still make a bankruptcy order but where the court is satisfied that an appeal is bona fide, it should order the petition to be stayed generally with liberty to apply. The court has power to go behind a judgment debt and to enquire into the consideration for such debt. If the petition is based on non-compliance with a statutory demand, the debtor can still dispute liability for the debt and the fact that no application has been made to set aside the demand does not mean that the debtor cannot raise this defence. It is for the court to judge whether the dispute as to the amount claimed in the demand is bona fide or not.

It is now often the case that an application for an interim order in connection with a voluntary arrangement will come before the court at the same time as the bankruptcy petition. Provided that the papers are in order, an interim order should be made and the bankruptcy petition adjourned. The practice of some courts of making a bankruptcy order and thereafter an interim order which has the effect of staying the bankruptcy proceedings is not a proper exercise of the court's discretion. For more regarding voluntary arrangements, see chapter 3 below.

2.4.13 The order The bankruptcy (Form 6.25 in Sched 4 to the Rules) is prepared by the court (r 6.33). The order is sent by the court to the Official Receiver, who must send one to the debtor and advertise the making of the order in the local newspaper and the *London Gazette*.

If the petition is dismissed, the petitioner must prepare the order in Form 6.22.

2.5 Debtor's petition

2.5.1 Grounds The debtor may present his own bankruptcy petition on the ground that he is unable to pay his debts (ss 264(1)(*b*) and 272(1)). The petition must be accompanied by a statement of affairs in the prescribed form (Form 6.28). Copies of this form can be obtained from the court and the Official Receiver.

2.5.2 Which court? The same rules as to jurisdiction which apply to creditors' petitions apply also to debtors' petitions. However, under r 6.40(3), except in the case where the High Court is the appropriate court, if it is more expedient for the debtor he can present his petition to one of the alternate county courts specified in Sched 2 to the Rules as being in relation to the debtor's own county court the nearest full time court. These alternate courts are set out in Appendix 1.

2.5.3 Form The prescribed form of debtor's petition is Form 6.27 in Sched 4 to the Rules. Copies of this form can be obtained from the court and Official Receiver's offices.

2.5.4 Issue When issuing a debtor's petition, the following are required:

- the petition (and three copies);
- a statement of affairs (and two copies);
- a receipt for the deposit—currently £135; and
- a fee—currently £20.

One copy of the petition is returned to the debtor endorsed with the hearing date. The court forwards the remaining copy petitions and statements of affairs to the Official Receiver and any insolvency practitioner appointed under s 273 (see below). In cases of urgency, the debtor can deliver documents direct to the Official Receiver if the court directs (r 6.42(6)).

2.5.5   Hearing of the petition   The court may make a bankruptcy order on the hearing. If the liabilities of the estate are less than the small bankruptcies level (currently £20,000), the court may issue a certificate for the summary administration of the estate. Alternatively, the court may appoint an insolvency practitioner to prepare a report under s 273. If the debts owed by the debtor are less than the small bankruptcies level and the assets are above the minimum level, currently £2,000, then the court must *not* make a bankruptcy order but should instead appoint an insolvency practitioner to prepare a report under s 273. It is then the duty of the insolvency practitioner to report to the court on whether or not the debtor is willing to enter into a voluntary arrangement and on whether a meeting of the debtor's creditors should be convened. If the insolvency practitioner does submit a report which suggests that a voluntary arrangement might be entered into by the debtor, the court can make an interim order under s 252 so as to facilitate the implementation of this voluntary arrangement. For more about voluntary arrangements, see chapter 4 below.

2.5.6   Making the order   The court draws up the bankruptcy order and serves copies on all concerned including the bankrupt. The Official Receiver notifies the Chief Land Registrar, gazettes the order and advertises it in a local newspaper. The court can also issue a certificate of summary administration (see above). The certificate can be revoked on the court's own motion or on application to the Official Receiver if it appears that it should not have been issued. The effect of the certificate being issued is that there is no obligation on the Official Receiver to investigate the debtor's conduct and the debtor can expect an automatic discharge at the end of two years rather than three.

2.6   Pre- and post-bankruptcy order matters

2.6.1   Restrictions   If a person is made bankrupt, any disposition of his property (including payments made by him) after the date of the presentation of the petition is void (unless made with the consent of the court) (s 284(1) and (3)). Excepted are recipients who acted in good faith, for value, without notice of the bankruptcy petition and before the bankruptcy order was made (s 284(4)(a)). Notice of a statutory demand is not the same as notice of a petition for the purposes of s 284(4) though notice that the statutory demand has not been complied with might constitute lack of good faith, as suggested in *Re Dalton* [1963] Ch 336.

Once a bankruptcy petition has been presented, any court *may* stay any action or other legal process against the debtor or his property (s 285(1)). The granting of a stay is discretionary. Either the bankruptcy court or the court in which proceedings are pending can order the stay. Once a bankruptcy order has been made, a creditor has no remedy against the person or property of the bankrupt and may not commence any action against him without leave of the court (s 285(3)). This rule is subject to the right of a landlord to continue with distress for rent commenced prior to the bankruptcy order and the right of a creditor to retain the benefit of executions completed by seizure and sale before the making of the bankruptcy order.

A secured creditor is not affected by these provisions and can enforce his security though he cannot take any action in connection with any unsecured shortfall.

2.6.2 Interim receivership If it is necessary to protect the debtor's property prior to the hearing of the bankruptcy petition, the court can, on the application of either the debtor or a creditor, appoint the Official Receiver as interim receiver (s 286(1)). If an insolvency practitioner has been appointed under s 273 (to consider whether a voluntary arrangement would be more appropriate in the case of a debtor's petition), that insolvency practitioner may be appointed interim receiver. The court will specify the powers which the interim receiver is to have. A deposit for the costs of the interim receiver may be required from the creditor making the application. Between the making of the bankruptcy order and the time when the bankrupt's estate vests in a trustee (be it the Official Receiver or an insolvency practitioner) the Official Receiver is the receiver and manager of the estate. He is only entitled to sell perishable goods and any other goods whose value is likely to diminish if not disposed of (s 287(2)) and is not obliged to do anything which might involve his incurring expenditure unless directed to do so by the Secretary of State or so authorised by a meeting of creditors.

2.6.3 Rescission and annulment Every court having jurisdiction in bankruptcy may review, rescind or vary any order made by it (s 375(1)). If the proceedings have been transferred from one court to another after the making of the bankruptcy order, the transferee court can also exercise such powers. The court will not rescind an order simply because the debtor asks for it and the petitioning creditor or the general body of creditors also consent. The court has an obligation to look into all the circumstances before rescission.

The court may annul a bankruptcy order if it appears to the court either that the order ought not to have been made or that the debts and expenses of the bankruptcy have all been paid or secured to the satisfaction of the court since the making of the order (s 282(1)). The first of these alternatives requires some irregularity or invalidity in the proceedings. The second requires the court to be satisfied that all the debts have been paid in full and not merely that the debts have been bought by a third party for less than their value. If there are some disputed debts or untraced creditors, the court may require security in the form of a bond or money in court to cover these potential creditors. The jurisdiction conferred on the court to annul a bankruptcy is discretionary and an order may be refused if, having regard to the conduct of the bankrupt, it seems right to do so. In *Re Taylor ex parte Taylor* [1901] 1 KB 744, the bankrupt did not disclose all his assets and merely handed to the Official Receiver a portion of his assets sufficient to pay his debts and costs in full. Annulment was refused.

Rescission and annulment have the effect of 'cancelling' the proceedings, but any criminal proceedings brought against the bankrupt are not brought to an end.

2.6.4 Statement of affairs

In all cases where a bankruptcy order is made, the bankrupt is obliged to submit a statement of affairs. In the case of a debtor's own petition, the statement of affairs will have been included with the papers lodged at court at the time the petition was issued. The statement must be submitted to the Official Receiver within 21 days of the making of the bankruptcy order (s 288(1)) or such longer time as the court or the Official Receiver may allow (s 288(3)). The statement must contain full particulars of the bankrupt's creditors, debts and other liabilities and of his assets together with such information as may be prescribed. Form 6.33 is prescribed for the statement of affairs (Sched 4). The Official Receiver is obliged to give the bankrupt copies of this form. The statement of affairs must be verified by an affidavit delivered together with a copy (r 6.60(2) and (3)).

If the bankrupt himself cannot prepare a proper statement of affairs, the Official Receiver may employ someone at the expense of the estate to assist him or may authorise an allowance out of the estate towards the expense incurred by the bankrupt in employing someone to assist in its preparation. The Official Receiver must receive an estimate from the bankrupt of the likely costs to be incurred and only a named person, approved by the Official Receiver, can be authorised to do the work (r 6.63). If the bankrupt fails without reasonable excuse to lodge a statement of affairs then he is guilty of contempt of court.

The Official Receiver can require the bankrupt to furnish accounts relating to three years prior to the bankruptcy and the court can order that accounts for earlier years be submitted also. The Official Receiver can also require the bankrupt to give further information explaining or amplifying anything contained in his statement of affairs or accounts (r 6.66).

2.6.5 Public examination

There is now no automatic public examination of a bankrupt and if the Official Receiver wants the bankrupt to be publicly examined, then he must make application to the court (s 290). A creditor can also ask the official Receiver to make application to the court for a public examination to be held, provided that the creditor is supported by not less than half in value of all the creditors of the bankrupt. The procedure for making this request is set out in r 6.173. If the bankrupt fails to attend his public examination, he is guilty of contempt of court (s 290); but if he is unfit to undergo a public examination, he can make application to the court for the examination to be conducted in some other manner (r 6.174). At the public examination, the Official Receiver, the trustee and any creditor who has tendered a proof of debt can ask questions and can, with the approval of the court, appear by solicitor or counsel or authorise in writing another person to question the bankrupt on his behalf (r 6.175).

The bankrupt must take the oath and answer all the questions as the court may put or allow to be put. He may employ a solicitor or counsel at his own expense for the purpose of enabling him to explain or qualify any answers given. The bankrupt is not entitled to refuse to answer questions on the ground that he may incriminate himself but, if criminal proceedings have been commenced against the bankrupt and the court is of the opinion that the continuation of the examination would be likely to prejudice a fair trial of those proceedings, the examination may be adjourned (r 6.175). The purpose of questioning is to ascertain if there are any further assets or rights for the creditors or any protection to the public which might be obtained by the answers. A written record of the proceedings is taken and ultimately has to be signed by the bankrupt and verified by affidavit at a later date. This written record can be used as evidence against the bankrupt in any proceedings against him though not against third parties.

The public examination may be adjourned from time to time either to a fixed date or generally (r 6.176). Where the examination is adjourned generally, the Official Receiver may, there and then and without prior notice to the bankrupt, make application under s 289(3) for the relevant period for the automatic discharge of the bankrupt to cease to run (r 6.176(4)). If such an application is not made at this time, it can be made by the Official Receiver at a later stage.

2.7 Appointment of trustee and creditors' committee

2.7.1 Who may be appointed trustee?
The trustee can be appointed by a general meeting of the creditors (except where there is in force a certificate of summary administration), by the court (where a bankruptcy follows on a voluntary arrangement) or by the Secretary of State (where the creditors have failed to appoint a trustee and the Official Receiver considers one appropriate). No person can be appointed a trustee unless he is an authorised insolvency practitioner (s 292). Two or more trustees can be appointed to act jointly.

2.7.2 Calling the creditors' meeting
Unless there is in force a certificate for summary administration, the Official Receiver must decide within 12 weeks after the making of the bankruptcy order whether or not to summon a meeting of creditors for the purpose of choosing someone to be the trustee (s 293(1)). If he decides that a meeting should be called, that meeting must be held

not more than four months from the date of the bankruptcy order and 21 days' notice must be given to all creditors (r 6.79). Notice must also be given by advertisement in a local newspaper and the *London Gazette*. In any case, if the Official Receiver receives a request from a creditor supported by at least 25 per cent in value of all the other creditors, he must call a meeting (s 294). That meeting must be held within three months (r 6.79).

In fixing the venue of the meeting, the Official Receiver must have regard to the convenience of those who are to attend and meetings must be held between 10 am and 4 pm on business days unless the court orders otherwise. The notice convening a meeting must include a form of proxy to enable creditors who cannot attend the meeting to appoint someone else to attend on their behalf. The bankrupt can be required by the Official Receiver to attend the meeting (r 6.84).

2.7.3 Rules governing meetings   The following rules apply to all meetings of creditors:

- *Chairman*—The Official Receiver acts as chairman at the first meeting and the trustee at all other meetings.
- *Resolutions*—Resolutions are deemed to be passed on a majority in value of the creditors present personally or by proxy who vote in favour of it (r 6.88).
- *Quorum*—There must be a quorum otherwise the meeting is adjourned. The quorum is at least one creditor in person or by proxy. If the chairman by himself or with one creditor would constitute a quorum and the chairman is aware that other creditors intend to attend, the meeting must not commence until at least 15 minutes after the appointed time (r 12.4A(4)).
- *Adjournments*—If the meeting has to be adjourned, it must be adjourned for not more than 21 days.
- *Proof of debt*—No creditor can vote at any meeting unless he has lodged proof of debt in the appropriate form (Form 6.37 in Sched 4) and the claim has been admitted for the purpose of entitlement to vote (r 6.93(1)). Creditors cannot vote if their debts are unliquidated or secured, though a partially secured creditor can value his security and vote for his unsecured shortfall. The chairman may reject a proof for voting purposes but that decision is subject to appeal (r 6.94). If the chairman is in doubt as to the validity of a claim, he should mark the proof of debt accordingly and allow the creditor to vote subject to his vote being subsequently declared invalid if the objection is sustained (r 6.94(3)). If the validity of this particular proof had a material effect on the outcome of the meeting, the court may order a further meeting.
- *Chairman to propose resolutions*—Where the chairman holds a proxy requiring him to vote for a particular resolution, he must propose that resolution if no one else does so unless he considers that there is good reason for not doing so (r 6.89).

2.7.4 Proxies A creditor may vote either by person or in proxy. Only a sole trader or other individual can vote in person. All other creditors have to use proxies to give authority to someone to attend the meeting and vote on their behalf. A company can authorise a person to attend creditors' meetings and vote on its behalf, by a resolution under s 375 of the Companies Act 1985. A copy of the authority must either be under the seal of the company or be certified as a true copy by a secretary or a director (r 8.7).

There is no appeal against the decision of the chairman to declare invalid a proxy that has been lodged and so disentitle that creditor's representative from voting, but it is open to the creditor affected to apply to the court for the chairman's decision to be reversed and for a new meeting to be held.

Forms of proxy must be sent out with notices summoning meetings. Only the prescribed forms may be used. The prescribed form is Form 8.4 in Sched 4.

A proxy can either be a general proxy—allowing the proxy holder to use his discretion on voting—or a special proxy—requiring the proxy holder to vote for or against any specified resolution. The Official Receiver may be appointed as proxy holder by a creditor. Proxies intended for use at a meeting must be lodged by the time stated in the notice summoning the meeting. No improper solicitation may be used in obtaining proxies or in procuring an appointment as trustee. If such improper solicitation has been used, no remuneration will be allowed to the person who has benefited by reason of such solicitation.

A proxy holder may not vote in favour of a resolution which would place him in a position to receive any remuneration out of the estate unless the proxies are in the form of special proxies, provided that if the proxy holder himself has signed the proxy in his own favour, he produces to the chairman written authorisation from the principal sufficient to show that he was authorised to sign (r 8.6(1A)).

2.7.5 Business at first meeting The primary purpose of the first meeting is to appoint a trustee. No resolution can be proposed which has as its object the appointment of the Official Receiver as trustee (r 6.80(2)). The Official Receiver will become the trustee only if no other nominations are put forward and the Official Receiver does not ask the Secretary of State (under s 296) to appoint another person as trustee. The meeting may resolve to establish a creditors' committee (see also s 7 below). Unless a creditors' committee has been established, the meeting can specify the terms of the trustee's remuneration. No person can be appointed as trustee unless he is a qualified insolvency practitioner. The chairman of the meeting must certify the appointment of the trustee but cannot do so unless the person appointed has provided him with a written statement that he is a qualified insolvency practitioner and consents to act (r 6.120(2)). A trustee's appointment is effective from the date on which the certificate of appointment is received from the Official Receiver.

2.7.6 Change of trustee In order to resign, the trustee must call a meeting of creditors and give an account of his administration (r 6.26). A trustee may resign only because of ill-health, his ceasing to be a qualified insolvency practitioner or because of some conflict of interest. If there is no quorum at the meeting of creditors to consider the trustee's request to be allowed to resign, his resignation is deemed to have been accepted. Notice of the meeting must be given to the Official Receiver and he must be informed of the outcome.

During any vacancy of the post of trustee, such as that caused by death, the Official Receiver becomes the trustee (s 300(2)). He must then decide whether or not to convene a further meeting of creditors having regard to the state of the administration of the estate. A trustee other than the Official Receiver can be removed by resolution of creditors at a meeting duly summoned of which proper notice has been given (s 298(1)). The court may remove a trustee on the application of an interested person and the Secretary of State may remove a trustee, having given the trustee notice of his intention to do so so that representations against his removal can be made (r 6.133).

2.7.7 Role and membership of committee Creditors may resolve to establish a committee, though a committee cannot be established at any time when the Official Receiver is trustee. Any creditor other than a secured creditor is eligible to be a member of the committee providing that he has lodged a proof of debt which has not been disallowed. A body corporate can be a member of the committee but it may act through a representative. A creditors' committee must consist of at least three and not more than five members.

The role of the committee is primarily supervisory, though one of its functions is to determine the trustee's remuneration (r 6.138(3)). It can determine that the trustee should be paid a percentage of the value of the assets realised or distributed or on a time basis. No resolution of the committee may override the general rule that where a trustee has used improper solicitation to obtain proxies so as to procure his appointment no remuneration is allowable to him.

The trustee is under a duty to report to the committee all matters of concern to them with respect to the administration of the estate (r 6.152(1)). The trustee must send a report to every member of the committee from time to time (not less than once every six months or as and when directed by the committee, though not more often than once every two months) (r 6.163). The first meeting of the committee must take place within three months of its establishment and thereafter within 21 days of a request for a meeting by a member of a committee. The trustee chairs the meeting. The quorum is two (r 6.155). The trustee can seek to obtain the agreement of the committee to a resolution by sending to every member a copy of the proposed resolution (r 6.162(1)). In the absence of a request for a meeting to consider the resolution, the resolution is deemed to have been passed if and when the trustee is notified in writing by a majority that they concur.

A committee member may resign by notice to the trustee and his membership is automatically terminated if he becomes bankrupt or is absent from three consecutive meetings (unless it is resolved that this rule should not apply at the third meeting) or if he ceases to be or is found never to have been a creditor (r 6.158). Vacancies of the committee need not be filled. If the majority of the remaining members agree, the trustee can either appoint some other creditor to be a member of the committee if the majority of the remaining members agree or convene a meeting of creditors to appoint someone else. No member of the committee who is a representative or associate nor anyone who has been a member of the committee within the last 12 months may enter into any transaction whereby he receives out of the estate any payment for services given or goods supplied or obtains any profit from the administration or acquires any asset forming part of the estate (r 6.155(2)) except with the leave of the court or with the prior sanction of the committee.

Members of the committee are entitled to receive their expenses for attending meetings but otherwise are not entitled to any payment out of the estate. Where there is no committee and the trustee is other than the Official Receiver, the functions of the committee are performed by the Official Receiver on behalf of the Secretary of State.

The trustee can only exercise certain powers with the sanction of the creditors' committee. The matters requiring sanction are set out in Sched 5 to the Act. These powers include the right to carry on the business of the bankrupt, to prosecute or defend any legal actions and to compromise any dispute with one of the bankrupt's creditors or debtors.

2.8 Debts and dividends

2.8.1 Types of creditor
There are four classes of creditor—secured, preferential, unsecured and deferred.

A secured creditor is not given any special priority by the Act or the Rules but can rely upon his security. He may, with the agreement of the trustee and leave of the court, at any time alter the value which he has in his proof of debt placed upon his security though if he petitioned for the debtor's bankruptcy or has voted in respect of his unsecured balance, he may only revalue his security with leave of the court (r 6.115).

If a secured creditor omits to disclose his security in his proof of debt, he must surrender it for the general benefit of creditors unless the court relieves him on the ground that omission was by mistake. A trustee may redeem the security of the value placed upon it by the creditor if he so wishes and a secured creditor has the right to call upon the trustee to elect whether or not to exercise this power.

Preferential debts are defined in s 386 and Sched 6 to the Act. They consist primarily of taxes such as PAYE, VAT, and social security contributions. Amounts due to employees for wages for the four months prior to the making of the bankruptcy order but not exceeding £800 for each employee are also preferential together with all arrears of holiday pay. If monies have been advanced by a third party to pay wages and holiday pay which otherwise would have been preferential debts, then the person who advanced the money becomes a preferential creditor for the amount advanced.

Unsecured creditors are the ordinary debts of the bankrupt which are neither secured nor preferential.

Deferred debts are those owed by the bankrupt to his spouse, the spouse being defined as at the date of the bankruptcy order. These debts rank after the preferential and ordinary unsecured creditors.

2.8.2 Provable debts

All claims by creditors against the bankrupt are provable whether they are present or future, certain or contingent, ascertained or sounding only in damages (r 12.3). Even unliquidated damages of tort are provable debts. However, fines or obligations under family or domestic court proceedings (ie, maintenance) are not provable debts (r 12.3(7)). The amounts due between husband and wife under the terms of a separation deed or agreement are provable debts since they are a contractual liability. Similarly, a lump sum order in divorce proceedings is a provable debt (*Curtess v Curtess* [1986] 1 WLR 422).

2.8.3 Proofs of debt

Every person claiming to be a creditor must submit his claim in writing to the Official Receiver or the trustee (r 6.96)—this is called proving his debt. A proof of debt must be in the prescribed form (Form 6.37 in Sched 4 or a substantially similar form. Proofs of debt forms must be sent out by the Official Receiver or trustee to every creditor who is known to him or identified in the statement of affairs.

The trustee may require proof of debt to be verified by affidavit in Form 6.39 in Sched 4 to the Rules. Such an affidavit can be sworn by the creditor before his own solicitor (r 7.57). A proof of debt must contain details of the creditor's name and address, the amount owing, the date of the bankruptcy order, whether interest and VAT is included, whether any part of the debt is preferential, how the debt was incurred and particulars of any security held and if so its value (r 6.98). If the debt was incurred in a foreign currency, the sterling equivalent must be stated as at the date of the bankruptcy order.

There is no time limit for the submission of proofs of debt but a creditor who has not proved his debt cannot benefit from any distribution of the bankrupt's assets nor can he vote at any meeting of creditors until proof has been lodged. Before declaring a dividend, the trustee must give notice of his intention to do so to all creditors of whom he is aware and who have not proved their debts (r 11.2(1)). The notice must specify the last date for proving, which must be not less than 21 days after the date of the notice. It must also state the trustee's intention to declare a dividend. The trustee must examine every proof of debt and admit it wholly or in part for dividend. If he rejects it, he must give his reasons in writing and inform the creditor concerned (r 6.104). The trustee cannot declare a dividend until he has examined every proof of debt. Acceptance of a proof of debt for voting purposes at the first meeting is not the same as acceptance by the trustee of a proof for dividend and the trustee is not bound by the earlier decision of the Official Receiver. If a creditor is dissatisfied at the decision of the trustee, the court may reverse that decision. No application to the court to vary the trustee's decision will be entertained unless it is made within 21 days from the date of service by the trustee of the notice of rejection with reasons (r 6.105). This time limit as with all other time limits is extendable by the court.

2.8.4   Interest   When a debt proved in a bankruptcy bears interest (contractual or statutory) the proof of debt can include interest up to the date of the bankruptcy order (r 6.113). If the debt does not include the right to interest, interest nonetheless can be claimed at the judgment rate up to the date of the bankruptcy order if the debt arose by virtue of a written instrument and in respect of a debt payable at a certain time after notice of intention to claim interest has been given (r 6.113). Interest on preferential debts would not appear to be preferential. If there is a surplus remaining after paying all proved debts (including interest on them up to the date of the bankruptcy order), it will be applied to the payment of interest on all proved debts (*pari passu*) at the greater of contractual or judgment rate.

2.8.5   VAT   A creditor whose claim includes an element of VAT can either prove for the whole amount of the claim (and pay to HM Customs and Excise the VAT element irrespective of whether or not he receives any dividend) or prove for the amount of his claim net of VAT and reclaim the VAT (Finance Act 1983 s 22(5)). No formalities are required to reclaim the VAT element of the debt owed by the bankrupt — the creditor is automatically entitled to VAT bad debt relief once he has written off the debt in his books and the debt is more than 6 months old.

2.8.6   Dividends   A trustee must give notice of his intention to pay a dividend to all creditors who proved their debts. The notice must include details of the amounts realised from the sale of assets, payments made by the trustee in the administration of the estate, the total amount distributed, the rate of dividend and whether any further dividends are to be expected. The trustee must not, except with the leave of the court, proceed to declare a dividend where there is pending an application to vary a decision of his on a proof of debt. If the trustee is unable to declare any or any further dividend, he must give notice to this effect to creditors. A creditor who has failed to lodge his proof of debt before an interim dividend is declared is not entitled to disturb that interim distribution but is entitled to receive a payment in priority to other creditors from further funds as available.

The trustee cannot be sued for a dividend but if he refuses to pay a dividend the court may order him to pay it together with, out of his own funds, interest at judgment rate and costs (s 325(1)).

On a final distribution, the trustee can ignore any creditors who have failed to lodge proofs of debt after receiving notice of the trustee's intention to declare a final dividend on a specified day (s 330).

2.9 Discharge from bankruptcy

2.9.1 Automatic discharge
In the case of a person who has not previously been bankrupt within the last 15 years or who has not been made criminally bankrupt, an automatic discharge at the expiry of three years from the making of a bankruptcy order is granted (s 279(1)). Where a certificate of summary administration is in force (only in the case of a debtor's petition where the liabilities do not exceed £20,000), the period of three years is reduced to two years (s 279(2)).

If the court is satisfied that the bankrupt has failed to comply with any of his obligations under the Act, it can order that the right to automatic discharge be suspended (s 279(3)). Any person made bankrupt before the Insolvency Act 1986 came into force was automatically discharged from bankruptcy on 29 December 1989 or will be so automatically discharged on the third anniversary after the adjudication of bankruptcy (whichever is the later) provided that he has not previously been bankrupt within the last 15 years (Sched 11 para 13(1) and (2). The Official Receiver can apply for time to cease to run.

2.9.2 Suspension of discharge
If the Official Receiver wants the right to automatic discharge to be suspended, he must file a report at court setting out why and the court will fix a date for the hearing of his application. The bankrupt can make application to the court for the suspension to be lifted. If such an application is made, the Official Receiver may serve a report on matters he considers should be drawn to the court's attention and the bankrupt may reply to these matters.

2.9.3 Application for discharge
If a person has been bankrupt previously (within the last 15 years) or has been made criminally bankrupt, the only way that he can be discharged from bankruptcy is to apply to the court for his discharge (s 280). No such application can be made until five years have elapsed since the making of a bankruptcy order. This period cannot be shortened. Those bankrupts entitled to an automatic discharge cannot use this procedure

to obtain their discharge earlier than at the end of three years (or two years in the case of a summary administration). On making an application for discharge, the bankrupt may be required to deposit with the Official Receiver sufficient money to cover his costs of the application.

2.9.4 Certificate of discharge Whenever a bankrupt is discharged the court must, at the request of the bankrupt, issue to him a certificate of his discharge and the date from which it was effective. The bankrupt can also require the Secretary of State to advertise his discharge in the *London Gazette* or in any other newspaper but he must be responsible for the costs of the advertisement (r 6.220).

2.9.5 Effect of discharge When a bankrupt is discharged he is released from all obligations in respect of his pre-bankruptcy liabilities. There are exceptions to the rules stated above in the case of obligations incurred by fraud, fines, damages for negligence in respect of personal injuries, obligations arising under any order made in family proceedings and non-provable debts (s 281).

2.10 Bankruptcy offences

2.10.1 Liability to prosecution Bankruptcy itself is not a crime but there are offences set out in the Insolvency Act for which a bankrupt can be prosecuted. Even after a bankrupt has obtained an annulment of the bankruptcy, criminal proceedings, once begun, can be continued against him but new proceedings cannot be brought. Likewise after discharge, proceedings already begun can be continued. Prosecution for an offence of being a director of a limited company while an undischarged bankrupt can be commenced even after annulment or discharge. Only the Secretary of State or the Director of Public Prosecutions can bring criminal proceedings. The maximum punishment for each offence under the Insolvency Act is set out in Sched 10 to the Act and is seven years' imprisonment or fine or both (on indictment) or six months' imprisonment or a fine of £1,000 (or both) (summary). A lower maximum of two years' imprisonment is provided for offences under ss 354, 357, 358, 360, 361 and 362 and also under s 11 of the Company Directors Disqualification Act.

2.10.2 Defence of innocent intention (s 352) If the bankrupt can show that he had no intent to defraud or to conceal the true state of his affairs, this constitutes a defence to many of the criminal offences.

2.10.3 Non-disclosure If the bankrupt does not disclose all his assets to the Official Receiver or fails to inform him of any disposal which might be set aside, he commits an offence. The defence of innocent intention is available.

2.10.4 Concealment of property (s 354) If the bankrupt fails to deliver to the Official Receiver or his trustee all his assets or if he conceals any debt due to or from him or any property with a value of more than £500, he commits an offence. Section 354 applies retrospectively to the concealment of any debt or property of at least £500 in the 12 months prior to the presentation of the bankruptcy petition. Section 352 (above) is available as a defence.

2.10.5 Explanations (s 354(3)) If the bankrupt fails to account for the loss of any substantial part of his property incurred in the 12 months before the petition was presented against him, he commits an offence. Section 352 is *not* available as a defence.

2.10.6 Books and papers (s 355) If the bankrupt fails to deliver up all his books, papers and other records or prevents the production of any records or conceals or destroys them, he commits an offence. An offence is committed if any of these actions is carried out by the bankrupt in the 12 months prior to the presentation of the petition. Section 352 is available as a defence.

2.10.7 False statements (s 356) If the bankrupt makes any false statement then he commits an offence. Section 352 is *not* available as a defence.

2.10.8 Fraudulent disposal of property (s 357) If the bankrupt makes any gift or transfer of property within five years prior to the presentation of the petition, an offence is committed. If the bankrupt has concealed or removed any part of his property within the five months before or after judgment has been obtained against him, an offence is also committed. Section 352 is available as a defence.

2.10.9 Absconding (s 358) The bankrupt commits an offence if he leaves or attempts to leave or makes any preparation to leave England and Wales with any property of not less than £500 value in the six months prior to the presentation of the petition. Section 352 is available as a defence.

2.10.10 Fraudulent dealing with property obtained on credit (s 359) The bankrupt commits an offence if within 12 months before the presentation of the petition, he disposed of any property which was obtained on credit and in respect of which money was still owing. Section 352 is available as a defence. It is also an offence for anyone to acquire property from a bankrupt in the same period knowing the true circumstances.

2.10.11   Obtaining credit or engaging in business (s 360)   The bankrupt commits an offence if he obtains credit of more than £250 without disclosing the fact that he is a bankrupt or if he engages in business in a name other than his own and without disclosing his true name to anyone from whom credit is obtained. Someone who has been made bankrupt in Scotland or Northern Ireland is also guilty of this offence if he seeks to obtain credit in England and Wales. Section 352 is *not* available as a defence.

2.10.12   Failure to keep proper accounts (s 361)   A bankrupt commits an offence if he fails to keep proper accounting records within two years prior to the presentation of the petition against him. An offence is not committed if the total of the bankrupt's liabilities is less than £20,000 or if the bankrupt proves that in the circumstances in which he carried on business, the omission to keep proper accounts was honest and excusable. Section 352 is *not* available as a defence.

2.10.13   Gambling (s 362)   A bankrupt commits an offence within two years prior to the presentation of the petition against him, if he materially contributed to his insolvency by gambling or hazardous speculations. Section 352 is *not* available as a defence.

2.10.14   Being a director of a limited company   It is an offence under the Company Directors Disqualification Act 1986 s 11 for a bankrupt to act as a director of or to be directly or indirectly concerned in the management of a limited company without the leave of the court. The definition of being concerned in the management of a limited company is very wide and is intended to be so. If in doubt, a bankrupt should apply to the court for permission to do that which he wishes to do vis à vis a company. It is also an offence to aid and abet someone to contravene this section. Civil liability for all debts incurred is also imposed on the disqualified person and anyone who aids or abets him.

2.10.15   Miscellaneous   A bankrupt is liable to be arrested and punished for contempt of court if he fails to do as he was directed by the court. The transcript of a bankrupt's public examination may be used against him in criminal proceedings.

2.11   Criminal court action

2.11.1   Criminal bankruptcy   The provisions of the Powers of the Criminal Courts Act 1973 giving the High Court and Crown Court the power to make a criminal bankruptcy order against an offender were repealed by the Criminal Justice Act 1988. If a person has been made bankrupt as a result of a criminal bankruptcy order, he still has no automatic right to a discharge from that bankruptcy. The person made criminally bankrupt has to make application to the court for his discharge and such an application cannot be made until the expiration of five years after the making of the bankruptcy order.

2.11.2 Confiscation order Where a person has been convicted of an offence before the Crown Court or the magistrates' court and it appears to the court that loss or damage (not attributable to personal injury) has been suffered by one or more persons of at least £10,000, the court may make a confiscation order (Criminal Justice Act 1988 s 71). To arrive at the sum of £10,000 there can be included all offences taken into consideration as well as the subject of the substantive charges.

2.11.3 Restraint order The court can make a restraint order to prevent an accused from disposing of his property prior to the conclusion of the criminal proceedings (Criminal Justice Act 1988 s 77).

2.11.4 Receiver The court can appoint a receiver to realise the property of the offender in such manner as it directs and can impose a charge on that property until payment is obtained (Criminal Justice Act 1988 s 80).

2.11.5 Effect of bankruptcy If the offender is adjudged bankrupt, any property subject to a restraint order and any proceeds of sale of property realised by a receiver are excluded from the bankrupt's estate (s 84(1)). If the offender is adjudged bankrupt before the making of the restraint order or the appointment of a receiver, then s 84(1) does not apply (s 84(2)). No order can be made under s 339 or s 423 (avoidance of transactions at an undervalue or transactions defrauding creditors) while criminal proceedings which might result in a confiscation order, restraint order or charging order are pending (s 84(6)). If a trustee in bankruptcy sells property which unbeknown to him is subject to a restraint or charging order, he will not be liable for any loss resulting from its disposal (unless he was negligent) and he is also entitled to a lien on the proceeds of sale for his expenses in connection with the disposal (s 87).

2.12 Trustee's powers

2.12.1 Disclaimer The trustee may disclaim any property of the bankrupt which is onerous (s 315). Onerous property is defined as any unprofitable contract and any other property which is unsaleable or may give rise to a liability to pay money or perform any action on the part of the trustee. The trustee may disclaim notwithstanding that he has endeavoured to sell the property in question. There is no right to disclaim a contract affecting land simply because that contract is not beneficial to the estate without disclaiming the property itself. In order to disclaim, the trustee must give a notice in Form 6.61 (in Sched 4 to the Rules), file at court the notice and serve the same on the party affected.

There is no time limit within which the trustee can disclaim unless he has been served with notice by the person interested in the property requiring him to make a decision within 28 days (s 316). If the trustee disclaims a lease, the court can vest the property in any person claiming an interest in that property, the guarantor of any liability in respect of the property or, in the case of a dwelling-house, in the occupant (s 320). Disclaimer operates so as to determine the rights, interests and liabilities of the bankrupt and his estate in respect of a disclaimed property and discharges the trustee from all personal liability in respect of it. Disclaimer does not affect the rights and liabilities of third parties except so far as is necessary for releasing the bankrupt's estate and the trustee from any liability. Accordingly, a guarantor of a lease disclaimed by the trustee is released from any further liability as from the date of disclaimer (*Stacey v Hill* [1901] 1 KB 660) unless the bankrupt was only an assignee of the lease (*Warnford Investments Ltd v Duckworth* [1979] 1 Ch 127).

2.12.2   After-acquired and other property   Any property acquired by the bankrupt after a bankruptcy order has been made against him does not automatically vest in his trustee. The trustee may, however, claim that property for the benefit of the estate by giving notice within 42 days of first learning about the property in question (ss 307 and 308). The trustee has no right to claim the personal tools and domestic effects of the bankrupt whenever they may be acquired by the bankrupt. A bankrupt is authorised to continue in business after his bankruptcy providing that he informs everyone from whom he seeks credit of more than £250 that he is an undischarged bankrupt. The bankrupt is entitled to retain such tools, books, vehicles and other items and equipment as are necessary for his use personally by him in his employment, business or vocation (s 283(2)) but he is obliged to inform his trustee not less than once every six months of information relating to any business carried on by him (r 6.200).

2.12.3   Vesting of items of excess value   Where property is excluded from the bankrupt's estate because it comprises tools of trade or household effects under s 283(2), and the trustee is of the opinion that the value of these items exceeds the value of a reasonable replacement, the trustee can claim that property for the estate (s 308(1)). He may not do so unless he acts within 42 days of learning of the relevant circumstances (s 309).

2.12.4   Income payments order   The trustee can ask the court to make an order requiring the bankrupt to pay some of his income into the bankruptcy estate (s 310). The court must not require the bankrupt to make any payments from income so as to reduce his remaining income below what appears to be reasonably necessary for the domestic needs of himself and his family. Income for these purposes is widely interpreted and includes every payment in the nature of income, eg income from a trust. An income payments order may not be made after the bankrupt has obtained his discharge. It may not be effective after discharge unless its making was a condition of the discharge granted by the court or, if discharge was obtained by effluxion of time, where the court making the order directed it to continue after discharge subject to a maximum duration of three years (s 310(6)). Once an income payments order has been made, it can be varied or discharged on the ground of changed circumstances (r 6.193).

2.12.5 Mutual credit and set off An account must be taken of what sum is due from a bankrupt to another person where there have been mutual credits, mutual debts or other mutual dealings (s 323). The sum due from one party must be set off against the sum due from the other. Only the balance of the account is provable as a bankruptcy debt or is to be paid to the trustee as part of the bankruptcy estate. For set off to be allowed, there must be obligations on both sides giving rise to pecuniary liabilities so that an account can be taken and the balance struck. If the obligation on one side is to deliver goods and on the other is to pay a sum of money, there can be no set off (see *Eberle's Hotel Co v Jonas* [1887] 18 QBD 459). In *Rolls Razor v Cox* [1967] 1 QBD 552, set off between sales commission and the value of goods in the possession of the salesman was allowed.

Set off is mandatory and no contracting out is possible (*National Westminster Bank v Halesowen Presswork and Assemblies* [1972] AC 785). For set off to be successful, both liabilities must have arisen prior to the making of the bankruptcy order even though one of the debts may not be immediately due and enforceable until a time after the making of the bankruptcy order. There can be no set off between joint debts and separate debts. Debts must be due in the same right.

If a creditor has to repay money to the bankrupt's estate (eg because of a preference) he cannot set off against the sum he is required to pay any sum due to him from the bankrupt (see *Elgood v Harris* [1896] 1 QB 419 and *Re A Debtor* (No 82 of 1926) [1927] 1 Ch 410). Right to set off may exist even though one of the debts is secured. Where a creditor has both a preferential and a non-preferential claim in a bankruptcy, the amount due from him to the bankrupt must be set off rateably (see *Re Unit 1 Windows Ltd* [1985] 1 WLR 1383). It may be possible to set off against a debt due from one party, a contingent liability of the other (see *Carreras Rothamn Ltd v Freeman Matthews Treasurer* [1985] Ch 207 and *Re Charge Card Services* [1986] 3 WLR 697 and *Re A Debtor (No 66 of 1955)* [1956] 1 WLR 226). A Crown department can set off against a debt due by it any debt owed by the bankrupt to another

Crown department (*Re Cushla* [1973] 3 All ER 415 and *Re D H Curtis (Builders) Ltd* [1978] Ch 162).

2.12.6 The home Where the bankrupt has a spouse and the trustee wishes to obtain an order for sale of the property so as to realise the bankrupt's interest in that property, he must make application under the Matrimonial Homes Act 1983, s 1 or the Law of Property Act 1925, s 30, depending on whether the property is in the sole name of the bankrupt or in joint names. In deciding whether or not to allow the trustee to insist on a sale of the property, the court will take into account the interests of the creditors, the conduct of the spouse so far as contributing to the bankruptcy, the needs and financial resources of the spouse and children and all the circumstances of the case except the needs of the husband (s 336(5)). If the trustee's application is made within one year of the commencement of the bankruptcy, it will be presumed that the interests of the spouse outweigh all other interests. If the application is made after one year, then the presumption is the other way round. If the bankrupt has no spouse or children living with him, he has no right to remain in the property as against the trustee. If the bankrupt has no spouse living with him but has children under the age of 18, then similar considerations will apply as set out above.

The trustee in bankruptcy is in no better position than the bankrupt's spouse and will be subject to those authorities on the determination of each spouse's interest in the matrimonial home (see *Leake v Bruzzi* [1974] 1 WLR 1528, *Sutill v Graham* [1977] 1 WLR 819, *Gissing v Gissing* [1971] AC 886 and *Re Densham (a bankrupt)* [1975] 1 WLR 1519.

If for any reason the trustee has been unable to realise his interest in the home, he cannot conclude his administration without first considering whether it is appropriate to impose a charge on the bankrupt's property (s 332). The trustee may apply to the court for an order imposing a charging order on the property for the benefit of the estate. The charge would be for the equivalent of the deficiency in the estate. The procedure is set out in r 6.237 and the form of charging order is Form 6.79A in Sched 4 to the Rules.

2.12.7 General control of trustee There are many powers which the trustee can exercise only with permission of a creditors' committee. If there is no creditors' committee, the functions of the committee are exercised by the Secretary of State (s 302(2)). These powers are set out in s 314 and Sched 5 Pt I:

- carrying on the business of the bankrupt;
- instituting or defending any legal actions;
- compromising any claim of the bankrupt against a third party;
- compromising any dispute with the bankrupt's creditors.

The trustee may without the permission of the creditors' committee sell the bankrupt's property, exercise the rights and duties given to a trustee and deal with any property of which the bankrupt was entitled to a beneficial interest (s 314 and Sched 5 Pt II). If the trustee does anything which requires permission but without obtaining that permission, his actions can be ratified if the committee is satisfied that he acted in a case of urgency and applied for permission without undue delay (s 314(4)).

The trustee does not require sanction of the committee to employ a solicitor nor to dispose of property to an associate of the bankrupt. He should, however, give notice of his actions in both instances. The trustee has power to summon meetings of creditors so as to ascertain creditors' wishes. Creditors have the right to apply to the court for any decision of the trustee to be reversed or modified if they are dissatisfied with the trustee's decision (s 303).

The trustee's remuneration is determined by the creditors' committee but if the trustee is not satisfied with the decision of the committee, he can call a meeting of creditors to resolve otherwise (r 6.140). If still not satisfied, he can apply to the court (r 6.141). Similarly, creditors can apply to the court for the trustee's remuneration to be reduced even though it has been approved by the creditors' committee (r 6.142). The creditors' committee can require the trustee to insist that his solicitor's fees be taxed notwithstanding that he is of the opinion that they are reasonable (r 7.34(2)).

The trustee is subject to control by the court on the application of any creditor. He is not subject to control by the bankrupt himself unless there is a real prospect of there being a surplus after the payment of all creditors, claims and costs where the trustee's actions might diminish or eliminate this surplus. The trustee is subject to control by the Department of Trade on the monetary aspects of his administration. The trustee is required to pay all monies into the Insolvency Services Account at the Bank of England within 14 days of receipt of funds. He is also obliged to send to the Secretary of State an account of all his receipts and payments every year.

The court will not allow a trustee in bankruptcy (its officer) to retain or claim monies for distribution amongst the creditors when it would be inconsistent with natural justice to do so and something which an honest man would not do. This principle was first enunciated in *Re Condon ex parte James* [1874] 9 Ch App 609 and was restated in *Re Clark (A bankrupt)* [1975] 1 WLR 559. It was also considered in *Re T H Knitwear (Wholesale) Ltd* (1988) 4 BCC 102.

2.12.8 Adjustment of prior transactions The trustee has power to apply to the court for the reversal of certain transactions if those transactions were to the disadvantage of the estate and were carried out at a 'relevant time'. The relevant time is defined in s 341 in relation to transactions at an undervalue as being any time in the five years preceding the bankruptcy and in the case of preferences at any time in the period of six months prior to the bankruptcy, unless the recipient is an associate in which case the period is two years. If the transaction is one which is alleged to be at an undervalue and was entered into between two and five years before the bankruptcy or is a preference, it is deemed not to have been made at a relevant time unless the bankrupt was at that time insolvent or became insolvent in consequence of the transaction or preference (s 341(2)). In the case of a transaction at an undervalue entered into with an associate, it is presumed that these requirements have been satisfied.

Where a bankrupt entered into a transaction at an undervalue at a relevant time, the court can order the return of the benefit. For an order to be made, the court must be satisfied that the bankrupt had entered into a transaction. A positive act is required on his part. The court has to fix the invalidity point (with no consideration to full value). It has been held that the invalidity point was above the level of nominal or insignificant consideration but below the level of equality (*Re Abbott (a bankrupt)* [1983] Ch 45). The trustee should also use s 423 which replaced s 172 of the Law of Property Act 1925.

Where the bankrupt makes a preference at a relevant time, the recipient of a preference can be made to repay to the bankrupt's estate that which he received (s 340). The court must not make such an order unless it is satisfied the bankrupt was influenced in deciding to make the transfer of payment to the recipient by a desire to prefer him (s 340(4)) but it is sufficient if only one of the motives in making the payment was a desire to prefer. 'Desire' and 'intention' have to be distinguished and it is only the former which may cause the action to constitute a preference (*Re MC Bacon* [1990] BCC 78). It is presumed in the case of a preference in favour of an associate of a bankrupt that there was a desire to prefer (s 340(5)).

Where a person has been made bankrupt and has been a party to a transaction involving the provision of credit at an extortionate rate, the transaction can be reopened even if payment in full has been made (s 343). The onus of proving that the transaction was not extortionate is on the person who gave the credit.

Where a person engaged in business entered into a general assignment of book debts due to him and he was subsequently made bankrupt, the assignment is void against his trustee as against any book debts which had not been made at the date of the bankruptcy (s 344).

Where a creditor has, before the bankruptcy, issued execution against the goods or land of the bankrupt or attached any debt to him, he cannot retain the benefit of his actions as against the trustee unless execution or attachment was completed prior to the bankruptcy (s 346). The sheriff or bailiff is under an obligation to hold monies received for a period of 14 days and if he receives notice during that period that the debtor is being made bankrupt, then the monies must be handed over to the trustee (s 346(3)). A distraint (by a landlord) commenced prior to the bankruptcy but incomplete at the date of the bankruptcy can continue, but only so that the landlord receives a maximum of the rent due for the six-month period if accrued immediately before the bankruptcy (s 347). However, all forms of distraint are subject to the rule that if they have taken place in the three months prior to the making of the bankruptcy order, the proceeds of the distraint are charged for the benefit of the bankrupt's estate with the preferential debts.

No lien or other right to possession of any books, papers or other records of the bankrupt is enforceable against the bankrupt's trustee (s 349). A solicitor seeking to exercise a lien over his (bankrupt) client's papers may be required to produce them pursuant to s 366.

CHAPTER 3

INDIVIDUAL VOLUNTARY ARRANGEMENTS

3.1 Nature of an arrangement

An individual voluntary arrangement (IVA) is an arrangement between an individual debtor and his creditors whereby the creditors agree either to accept something less than 100p in the £ on their debts in full and final settlement or agree to some deferment of the time for payment of their debts. An IVA is essentially a private matter between the debtor and his creditors with the involvement of a nominee/supervisor acting in a similar way as a trustee in bankruptcy. While an IVA is being proposed, protection from the court is obtained for the debtor from his creditors.

3.2 Procedural steps

- The debtor obtains the consent of an authorised insolvency practitioner to act as nominee.
- The debtor submits to the nominee his proposals in writing.
- The debtor applies to the court for an interim order to give him protection from his creditors while the nominee considers his proposals.
- The nominee considers the debtor's proposals and comments on them.
- The court considers the proposals and the nominee's comments on them and directs whether or not a creditors' meeting should be held.
- The creditors' meeting takes place and the debtor's proposals are either accepted as made or modified or rejected.
- The court is informed at the outcome of the meeting and in the absence of any objections makes an order approving the IVA.
- The proposals are implemented by the supervisor.

3.3 The proposal

Only an individual debtor can make a proposal for an IVA—joint debtors such as partners cannot though they can enter into IVAs individually. Even someone who is an undischarged bankrupt can be the subject of an IVA.

The proposal on behalf of an undischarged bankrupt can be made either by the debtor himself or by his trustee. Deceased's insolvent estates cannot make proposals for an IVA. The consent of an authorised insolvency practitioner to act as nominee to the proposed IVA is required. Once consent has been obtained, the debtor must then submit to the nominee his proposals.

The Insolvency Act 1986 sets out the details that must be contained in the proposal. These include a short explanation as to why the debtor thinks an IVA is desirable and why the creditors may be expected to agree to it, details of all assets and liabilities (differentiating between secured, preferential and unsecured liabilities), whether there had been any transactions which could be reopened in bankruptcy (such as preferences) and what the cost of the IVA is likely to be.

For a precedent set of proposals for an IVA incorporating the standard conditions which apply to all IVAs, see Appendix 2, forms 1A and 1B.

3.4 The interim order

Whether or not the debtor needs protection from his creditors while the proposals are being considered, he must apply to the court for an interim order (s 253). As soon as the application for an IVA has been lodged, an application can be made ex parte for an order staying all actions against the debtor (s 254). Once this order has been made, any court in which proceedings are pending may stay those proceedings or allow them to continue on such terms as it thinks fit (s 254(2)). An application for an interim order should be made on Form 7.1 in Sched 4 to the Rules and the fee payable is £10. If the debtor is already bankrupt, the application should be made in the bankruptcy proceedings on Form 7.2. The application for an interim order must be accompanied by an affidavit setting out the reasons for making the application, details of all legal actions against the debtor and the fact that no previous application for an interim order has been made in the last 12 months (r 5.5(1)). The court to which such an application is made is the court which would have jurisdiction in bankruptcy (r 5.5A). The application must be served on the nominee, any creditor who has presented a bankruptcy petition against the debtor or, if the debtor is already bankrupt, his trustee (unless the trustee himself is the applicant).

If the court is satisfied after hearing all representations that an interim order should be made so as to facilitate the obtaining of approval to an IVA, an interim order will be made. It lasts only for 14 days but can be extended if the nominee asks for more time to file his report (r 5.6(4)). On the making of an interim order, the court must fix a date and venue for consideration of the nominee's report. This date will also be the date when the interim order ceases to have effect. The nominee's report must be filed two days before this hearing (r 5.10). Within seven days of delivering the proposal to his nominee, the debtor must also deliver a statement of his affairs (r 5.8). When the nominee lodges his report at court, he also delivers a copy of the debtor's proposals and statement of affairs.

3.5 The second hearing

The nominee's report and the debtor's statement of affairs will be before the court. The court has two alternatives. If the nominee has come to the conclusion that there is no point in pursuing the debtor's proposals, the court can discharge the interim order. If the court is satisfied that a meeting of creditors should be convened, it can extend the period for which the interim order is to have effect until after the meeting of creditors has been held and a report of that meeting can be filed at court. The court draws up the order and serves it on all parties. The meeting of creditors ordered by the court to be convened must be held between 14 and 28 days after the hearing (r 5.13).

3.6 The creditors' meeting

At least 14 days' notice must be given to all creditors. With the notice, there must be sent out a copy of the proposal, the statement of affairs and the nominee's comments on the proposal. There must also be sent out a form of proxy. The meeting should be held between 10 am and 4 pm on a business day at a place convenient to creditors (r 5.14). The nominee chairs the meeting and the meeting should be conducted in accordance with the usual rules as to meetings in insolvency matters. These include voting by reference to the value of debts. If the chairman is in doubt as to whether a vote should be allowed, he should mark it as objected to but allow the creditors to vote. If an appeal against the chairman's decision is made, a fresh meeting may be ordered if unfair prejudice or material irregularity has been caused. Any application to the court regarding the conduct of the meeting must be made within 28 days after the chairman's report has been filed (s 262). The appeal is dealt with by a High Court or circuit judge, not the registrar or district judge. For the proposal to be approved by creditors, there must be in excess of 75 per cent in value of the creditors present in person or by proxy voting in favour of the resolution (r 5.18(1)). Other resolutions at the meeting are passed by a simple majority. However, a resolution is not passed if, despite the majority of more than 75 per cent or 50 per cent in favour of it, those voting against the resolution include more than half in value of the creditors (excluding the votes of associates of the debtor). Similarly, the votes of creditors who were not given notice of the meeting but who suddenly appear are to be discounted. Secured creditors cannot vote but it would appear that partially secured creditors can vote for the unsecured part of their debts. The meeting can be adjourned from time to time but for a maximum of a total of 14 days. If there is not the requisite majority in favour of the proposals, the chairman can adjourn the meeting for another attempt to obtain approval to be made. If approval is not obtained at the second meeting, the debtor's proposal is deemed rejected. The meeting can put forward to the debtor modifications to his proposal (s 258) and the debtor has a choice either to agree to the modification or to stand by his original proposal (in which case he runs the risk that his proposal will not be approved). One common modification likely to be put forward is for someone other than the nominee to be supervisor.

The meeting must not approve any proposal which would affect the rights of secured creditors or preferential creditors to be accorded privileges granted to them by law, unless those classes of creditors concur. The chairman must report the decision of the meeting to the court (s 259). His report must include details of the resolutions carried (including any modifications) and a list of all creditors who are present or represented and how they voted. This report must be filed within four days of the meeting (r 5.2(2)).

3.7   The third hearing

There is a third hearing at court, at which the chairman's report to the creditors' meeting is considered. If the debtor's proposal has been declined, the court will discharge the interim order and leave the debtor to the mercy of his creditors. If the meeting has approved the debtor's proposal (with or without modification) no further order will be made by the court but the IVA is now in place. If the debtor was an undischarged bankrupt, the effect of approval to an IVA is that the bankruptcy order against him can be annulled but only once the period during which an application to challenge the chairman's decision could be made has expired (28 days) or after any application has been dealt with by the court (s 261) and subject to any order of the court as to the termination of the administration of the bankruptcy.

3.8   Procedure in non-bankruptcy cases

Where there are no bankruptcy proceedings pending, the procedure to obtain an interim order is simplified. Orders can be made at all three stages detailed in 3.4, 3.5 and 3.7 above, without any attendance at court. If the papers are in order and the nominee filed his report with the application for the interim order, the first and second stages can be combined in what is called a 'concertina order'. The procedure is set out in *Practice Direction (Bankruptcy No 1 of 1991)* [1992] 1 All ER 678.

3.9   Effect of approval

The approved arrangement binds every person who has been given notice of the meeting of creditors and was entitled to vote at it (whether or not actually present or represented). If a creditor has not been given notice of the meeting he can pursue his actions against the debtor including bankruptcy proceedings, though if the creditor could not, by virtue of the size of his debt, have materially affected the outcome of the meeting, the court may prefer to order that a fresh meeting be convened.

3.10   Implementation of the arrangement

Once the proposal has been approved, the debtor's assets must be handed over to the supervisor. The supervisor's duties include the realisation of the assets and the payment of a dividend to creditors. The supervisor must send out a notice to all creditors at the end of his administration giving a summary of all his receipts and payments.

3.11   Defaults

The debtor commits an offence if he makes any false representation with the object of obtaining approval of his creditors to an IVA (r 5.30). If the debtor defaults on any of his obligations under the IVA, the supervisor or any creditor can petition for his bankruptcy (s 276).

INSOLVENT PARTNERSHIPS

4.1 Governing rules

The rules relating to insolvent partnerships are set out in the Insolvent Partnerships Order 1986 (IPO). Schedules 1 and 2 to the IPO deal with modifications of the Insolvency Act 1986 in their application to insolvent partnerships. Schedule 3 sets out the prescribed forms. Insolvent partnerships are now treated as unregistered companies for the purposes of insolvency and are wound up accordingly. Individual partners can also be made the subject of individual bankruptcy orders or, if they are corporate members of a partnership, winding up orders. When a partnership is wound up, its assets are first used to meet partnership liabilities and then any surplus goes to meet any shortfall in the personal liabilities of the partners. Similarly, the assets of partners are first used to meet their personal debts and then any surplus is used to meet the shortfall in the partnership liabilities. Priority of debts is dealt with in art 10 of the IPO. Former partners in an insolvent partnership are liable to be disqualified from acting as directors of a company under the Company Directors Disqualification Act 1986 in the same way as directors of insolvent companies.

There are four alternative ways of dealing with insolvent partnerships:

- wind up the partnership;
- wind up the partnership and make the individual partners bankrupt (or in the case of a corporate partner, put into liquidation);
- make the individual partners bankrupt without making any insolvency order against the partnership as such; or
- make one or more of the individual partners bankrupt without making all of them bankrupt and without making any insolvency order against the partnership.

4.2 Winding up

To wind up an insolvent partnership, a winding up petition should be presented. If the petition is based upon a statutory demand, that demand must be in Form 4.1 in Sched 4 to the Insolvency Rules. There is no right to apply to have the demand set aside. The petition to wind up the insolvent partnership is the same as any petition to wind up an unregistered company, namely, Form 4.2 with such modifications as are required. The partners themselves can petition to wind up the partnership.

An individual partner can petition for the partnership to be wound up providing he obtains the leave of the court. Leave will be granted if he proves that either he has obtained judgment against the partnership for a debt of not less than £750, that he has taken all reasonable steps to enforce the judgment and has served the statutory demand in Form 2 in Sched 3 to the IPO.

4.3 Winding up and making individual partners bankrupt

To wind up the partnership and make the individual partners bankrupt, at least three petitions will be issued. One petition will be to wind up the partnership and the other petitions will be against two or more individual partners. The only ground for a petition against the partnership is that it is unable to pay debts as evidenced by the failure to pay a debt exceeding £750 and to comply with the statutory demand served on the partnership and the individual partners. The demand must be in Form 3 in Sched 3 to the IPO. If any of the partners are corporate partners, then the petition against the partner must be in Form 6 in Sched 3 and must be presented in the same court as the petition to wind up the partnership. The petition against the non-corporate partner must be in Form 7 in Sched 3 and must be presented in the same court as the winding up petition against the partnership. The petition against the individual partners can be heard only after the hearing of the petition against the partnership.

4.4 Partner's own petition for bankruptcy order

This is the equivalent of the debtor's petition in the case of a partnership. It is used where it is not desired to make a winding up order against the partnership even though the partnership is insolvent, and will be more often used in the case of small partnerships. The petition is Form 8 in Sched 3 and must be signed by all the partners or, if signed by only some of them, an affidavit must be sworn showing that the consent of all partners is given.

The petition must be presented to the court which would have jurisdiction to wind up the partnership (as opposed to the court having jurisdiction for the individual partner's bankruptcy). A statement of affairs is lodged at a later date. Unlike in individual debtor's bankruptcy petitions, there is no provision for the appointment of an insolvency practitioner to consider the possibility of a voluntary arrangement and no certificate of summary administration can be issued even if it is only a small case. After a bankruptcy order has been made against the partners, they can propose a voluntary arrangement to their creditors.

4.5 Petition against only some partners

A creditor owed money by a partnership can petition for a winding up of the partnership or petition for the bankruptcy of one or more of the partners, without joining the other partners. If such action is taken, then normal rules of bankruptcy procedure apply. In order to make a demand for payment against an individual partner, the creditor must be entitled to take enforcement action against that partner under the provisions of RSC Ord 81 r 5.

CHAPTER 5

DECEASED'S
INSOLVENT
ESTATES

5.1 Governing rules

The Administration of Insolvent Estates of Deceased Persons Order 1986 (SI No 1999) ('the Order') governs the administration of the affairs of deceased debtors. There are three situations where insolvency of an estate occurs:

- where administration has begun and it is discovered that the estate is insolvent;
- where a bankruptcy petition is pending against the deceased at the time of his death; or
- where no administration has been applied for when a creditor begins to press.

5.2 Where administration has begun

Where an estate is being administered and it is discovered that the estate is insolvent, the administration continues as before but the same provisions as are in force under the law of bankruptcy must be applied to the administration of the estate as regards the rights of creditors, provable debts and the priority of debts (art 4 of the Order). There are two exceptions to this general rule. First, reasonable funeral, testamentary and administration expenses have priority over all other debts. Secondly, it is not necessary for the executors to be licensed insolvency practitioners. Even where no grant of probate has been obtained but where an application for such a grant is pending, the above rules apply but the court dealing with the application for probate can transfer the proceedings (that is the application for a grant of probate) to the appropriate bankruptcy court which can make an insolvency administration order (art 5(3) and (4) and Sched 1 Pt II). The executors are under the same duty as a debtor as regards the submission of a statement of affairs in Form 7 in Sched 3 to the Order.

5.3 Petition pending at time of death

If there is a bankruptcy petition pending against a debtor at the time of his death, the bankruptcy proceedings can continue as if he were still alive subject to certain modifications (art 5). One modification is that reasonable funeral and testamentary expenses have priority over the preferential debts. If the bankruptcy petition has not been served at the date of death, it can be served on the debtor's personal representatives. The personal representatives can be required to do those things which the debtor himself is required to do under the bankruptcy rules.

5.4 Where no administration pending

Where there is no application for a grant of probate pending, a creditor can issue a petition for an insolvency administration order. The form of petition is Form 1 in Sched 3 to the Order. The petition must be served on the personal representatives of the deceased unless the court orders otherwise. The same rules as regards the minimum debt owing so as to found bankruptcy proceedings applies.

A creditor's petition for an insolvency administration order is Form 1 in Sched 3, unless the petition is presented following an individual voluntary arrangement in which case it is in Form 2 in Sched 3 or as a result of a criminal bankruptcy order where it is Form 3 in Sched 3. If the personal representatives of the deceased wish to petition, they must use Form 6 and they are required to lodge a statement of affairs at that time.

5.5 Modifications of general law

No actions by the personal representatives before the date of the insolvency administration order done in good faith will be invalidated. The insolvency administration order is deemed to have been made on the date of the death of the deceased though in fact made some time later. This provision would appear to catch any dispositions made after the deceased's death but art 5(2) and s 284(4) protect the recipients of any property from the estate who received it in good faith, for value without notice of presentation of the petition. Notwithstanding the death of the debtor, an investigation into his conduct and dealings can be made.

CHAPTER 6

COMPULSORY LIQUIDATIONS

6.1 Which court has jurisdiction

6.1.1 The High Court The High Court alone has jurisdiction in winding up proceedings if the issued share capital of the company is in excess of £120,000. Proceedings can either be commenced in the Companies Court in London or at one of the eight provincial district registries with chancery jurisdiction. Enquiries can be made of a central register to ascertain if a winding up petition is pending (see 6 below).

6.1.2 The county court The county court for the district in which the registered office of the company is situated also has jurisdiction in winding up proceedings provided that the issued share capital of the company does not exceed £120,000. Not all county courts have jurisdiction to entertain winding up proceedings. The same courts which have jurisdiction in bankruptcy have jurisdiction for winding up proceedings. See Appendix 1 for a list of county courts exercising bankruptcy jurisdiction (and accordingly winding up jurisdiction) in respect of their own areas and the areas of other county courts. In London, no county courts have bankruptcy jurisdiction and accordingly do not have jurisdiction for winding up proceedings.

6.1.3 The London Insolvency District The London Insolvency District comprises the City of London and the districts of certain county courts as set out in 2.2.3.

6.1.4 The wrong court If the petition is presented in the wrong court, the court can: transfer the proceedings to the correct court; or allow the proceedings to continue where they are, provided that court has winding up jurisdiction; or strike out the proceedings (r 7.12).

6.1.5 Transfer between courts Proceedings can be transferred from the High Court to a county court or vice versa at any time (s 118 and r 7.11). Transfer can be ordered either on the court's own motion or on the application of an interested party (r 7.13).

6.2 The statutory demand

6.2.1 What is a statutory demand? A statutory demand is a document prepared by a creditor in a prescribed form requiring the debtor company to pay the debt referred to in the demand or to secure or compound that debt to the satisfaction of the creditor within the period of three weeks after the demand has been served.

6.2.2 Why is a demand necessary? To found a petition for the winding up of the debtor company, the creditor must show that the debtor company appears to be unable to pay or to have any reasonable prospect of being able to pay the debt due to the petitioning creditor (s 123). One of the ways of showing that a debtor company appears to be unable to pay its debts is that it has been served with a statutory demand (claiming a debt of more than £750) and more than three weeks have elapsed since the demand was served on it and it has not complied with the demand (s 123). Two or more creditors can join together to bring the total debt due to over £750. A petition can be based, in the alternative, on an unsatisfied execution or on the inability of the company to pay debts (s 123(2))—in which case, there is no minimum debt requirement. See section 7.3.2.

6.2.3 Form There is a form of statutory demand prescribed by Sched 4 to the Rules, namely Form 4.1.

6.2.4 Completion

- *The debtor company*—the correct title and registered office should be given;
- *The creditor*—the full name and address should be stated;
- *The debt*—the amount must be stated and the consideration for it;
  —only a debt due at the date of the demand can be included;
  —if interest is being claimed, this should be shown separately and the rate charged shown and why it is being claimed;
- *Security*—a statutory demand can only be made for an unsecured debt and if the creditor holds any security he must specify what it is and put a value on it so that the amount of the unsecured portion of his debt can be identified.
- *Signature*—the demand must be signed by the creditor himself or by someone authorised on his behalf, such as his solicitor. If the creditor is represented by a firm of solicitors, the demand should be signed by an individual solicitor of that firm with the name, address, reference and telephone number of the firm added afterwards.
- *Time limits*—the prescribed period is 21 days.

6.2.5 Service   The demand must be left at the registered office of the company. Service by post (the normal method of service on a company) is not available (s 123(1)(a)) unless the debtor company acknowledges that the demand was received (*Re a Company (No 008790 of 1991)* [1991] BCLC 561).

6.2.6 Time for compliance   The debtor company appears unable to pay its debts if at least three weeks have elapsed since a demand was served on it and it has not complied with it. The day the demand was served and day a petition was presented are ignored for the purpose of calculating if the correct time has been allowed.

6.2.7 Defects in the demand   Rule 7.55, permitting a court to waive an irregularity or defect in insolvency proceedings, does *not* apply to statutory demands. If the amount claimed in the demand is overstated or part of the debt is disputed but there is still a minimum debt of £750 owing by the debtor company, then the demand can be relied upon.

6.3   Creditors' petitions

6.3.1 Which court?   The petition must be presented to either the High Court or the appropriate county court—see 7.1 above. If it is desired to petition against a company in respect of which there is already in force an administration order or a voluntary arrangement under Pt I of the Act, the winding up petition must be presented to the same court that dealt with the administration or voluntary arrangement (r 4.7(8)).

Enquiries can be made of the courts by telephone (071–936 7328 or 6790) to ascertain if a winding up petition is pending against the company.

6.3.2 Conditions for petitioning   A petition to wind up a company may be presented to the court if:

- the company has by special resolution resolved that the company be wound up by the court; or
- the company is unable to pay its debts; or
- it is just and equitable that the company should be wound up (s 122(1)).

The company is deemed unable to pay its debts if:

- a creditor has served a statutory demand for a minimum sum of £750 and the company has neglected to pay the sum or to secure or compound for it to the reasonable satisfaction of the creditor within three weeks after service; or
- execution or other process against the company is returned unsatisfied in whole or in part (no minimum debt requirement); or

- it is proved to the satisfaction of the court that the company is unable to pay its debts as they fall due (no minimum debt requirement) (s 123(1)).

A company is also deemed unable to pay its debts if its liabilities exceed its assets, taking into account contingent and prospective liabilities as well (s 123(2)).

It is not a precondition of being able to petition for the winding up of the company that a statutory demand has been served. If a debt is due and unpaid and cannot be disputed on some substantial ground, that is of itself evidence of inability to pay (*Cornhill Insurance v Improvement Services Limited* [1986] 1 WLR 115 and *Taylors Industrial Flooring v M & H Plant Hire (Manchester) Limited* (1990) BCC 44).

6.3.3 Form

There is a prescribed form of petition (Form 4.2) set out in Sched 4 to the Rules. The form of a contributories' petition is Form 4.14.

6.3.4 Completion

If two or more creditors are jointly petitioning, all their details must be given. Secured creditors must value their security and can only petition for the unsecured part of their debt or risk forfeiting their security. The petition must state the amount of the debt and the consideration for it. An assignee of a debt can petition but a garnishor of a debt cannot as he is merely the holder of a charge over a debt due to the garnishee. If a petition is based on a statutory demand, only the debt claimed in the demand can be included; any interest accrued since the demand was served cannot (*Practice Directions* [1987] 1 WLR 81 and 1424). It is necessary to complete the details of the company including its registered office, the date of incorporation, the authorised and issued share capital and principal objects.

6.3.5 Verification

Every petition must be verified by an affidavit (r 4.12(1), see Form 4.3). The affidavit must exhibit a copy of the petition and must be lodged at court at the time the petition is presented.

6.3.6 Issue

On issue of the petition the following are required:

- petition together with a sufficient number of copies for service on the company and any administrator, administrative receiver, supervisor or voluntary liquidator that are in office together with a copy for annexing to the affidavit of service;
- affidavit verifying the petition;
- receipt for the deposit payable to the Official Receiver (which the court will accept on his behalf—currently £270;
- the fee—currently £40.

All copies of the petition are sealed by the court and, except for one, are handed back to the petitioner. The petition is endorsed with details of the time, date and place of the hearing as fixed by the court.

6.3.7   Service   A sealed copy of the petition must be served personally on a director of the company or on a duly authorised person or by leaving it at the registered office (r 4.8). If none of these methods can be utilised, the court may allow substituted service on an ex parte application. An affidavit of service of the petition is required which must exhibit a sealed copy of the petition and, if substituted service has been ordered, a copy of that order. The form of affidavit of service is Form 4.4 in Sched 4 to the Rules. If substituted service has been utilised, Form 4.5 is required. If service is effected after 4 pm on a business day or after 12 noon on a Saturday, service is deemed to be effected on the next business day (RSC Ord 65 r 7). If a voluntary arrangement is in force, the supervisor must be served as well as the company unless it is the supervisor who is petitioning. If an administrative receiver has been appointed, he must also be served. If the company is already in voluntary liquidation, the voluntary liquidator must be served (r 4.10).

6.3.8   Advertisements   The petition must be advertised in the *London Gazette* not less than seven business days before the hearing and not less than seven business days after service (r 4.11). The form of advertisement is prescribed (Form 4.6). Advertisements should be sent to the *London Gazette* whose address is HMSO Publications Centre, 9 Elms Lane, London SW8 5DR. The current fee for the advertisement including VAT and one voucher copy of the *Gazette* is £23.73. The court has power to restrain the advertisement of a petition if it appears that there is a genuine dispute as to the debt alleged to be owing and harm would be caused to the company by allowing the petition to proceed.

6.3.9   Copies of the petition   All creditors, directors and shareholders of the company are entitled to be furnished with a copy of the petition within two days of requesting the same on payment of a fee (r 4.13).

6.3.10   Certificate of compliance   The petitioner or his solicitor must lodge at court at least five business days before the hearing a certificate showing compliance with the rules together with a copy of the advertisement in the *London Gazette*. The form of certificate is Form 4.7. If the certificate is not filed at court, the petition is liable to be dismissed (r 4.14).

6.3.11   Hearing of the petition   Petitions are initially set down for hearing before a registrar of the Companies Court in London or a district judge (of the High Court or county court) elsewhere. The registrar or district judge only has jurisdiction to hear unopposed petitions. If the petition is opposed it must be adjourned to a High Court or circuit judge. All the registrar or district judge can do is to investigate whether the reasons given for opposing could constitute sufficient grounds for refusing the winding-up order. Any creditor who intends to appear on the hearing of the petition must give notice to the petitioning creditor. The notice must state the amount of his debt and whether he intends to support or oppose the petition. The notice is in Form 4.9. The petitioning creditor must prepare a list of the creditors, if any, who have given notice of intention to appear. If no creditors have given any such intention, the list should be completed by writing 'none' across it. The list is prescribed in Form 4.10. The list is handed to the court clerk before the commencement of the hearing. It does not automatically follow that if more creditors in value oppose the petition than support it, that the petition will be dismissed. The courts will look at the 'quality' of the creditors supporting or opposing the petition and if the opposing creditors are associated with the company not as great weight may be attached to them. The courts are unwilling to adjourn a petition more than once since it must not be allowed to hang over the company's head indefinitely. If, however, insufficient time has elapsed since the company was served with the petition, the hearing must be adjourned. If the company intends to oppose the petition, its affidavit in opposition must be filed at court not less than seven days before the hearing and a copy must be sent to the petitioning creditor or his solicitor (r 4.18).

6.3.12 Substitution If the petitioning creditor has been paid his debt, the court may order that another creditor be substituted as petitioning creditor provided that that creditor has given notice of his intention to appear on the hearing and which is to prosecute the petition. The substituting creditor must also be owed a debt equal to the bankruptcy level, currently £750, and to have been in a position to present his own petition at the time the original petition was issued. If substitution is ordered, the petition will need amendment and it will have to be reserved. The hearing will therefore have to be adjourned. Rule 4.19 deals with substitution.

6.3.13 Withdrawal A petition cannot be withdrawn except with leave of the court. If a petition has been served but not advertised and the company consents, leave to withdraw will be given on an ex parte application provided that this is applied for at least five days before the hearing. Otherwise an application for leave to withdraw must be made at the hearing (r 4.15). Once the petition has been advertised application for leave to withdraw must be made at the hearing.

6.3.14 The hearing On the hearing of the petition the court may make a winding up order, adjourn the hearing conditionally or unconditionally or dismiss the petition (s 125(1)). The court's discretion is unfettered and it is not the case that if there is going to be no benefit to creditors in having a winding up, the petition will be dismissed (see *Re Television Parlour* (1988) 4 BCC 95 for a review of how the discretion will be exercised). The normal rule is, however, that if a majority of creditors in value support a petition then a winding up order will be made. Different considerations apply in the case of contributories' petitions where a winding up order will be refused if there is some other remedy available to the petitioners. Also, in cases where a compulsory winding up order is sought after voluntary liquidation has commenced, the court will look at all the circumstances and not merely take into consideration that the majority in value either want or do not want a winding up order to be made (see *Re Southard* [1979] 1 WLR 1198 and *Re Medisco Equipment Ltd* (1983) 1 BCC 98 and 944). An order that the costs of the petitioning creditor be paid by the company out of its assets will usually be made. These costs are a first charge on the company's assets and rank ahead of all other claims of secured creditors (including a fixed charge).

6.3.15 The order The winding up order itself (Form 4.11 in Sched 4) is drafted by the court. The draft order is sent by the court to the petitioning creditor or his solicitor who engrosses it and returns sufficient copies to the court for sealing. The court sends three sealed copies to the Official Receiver who in turn serves a copy on the company and the Registrar of Companies and arranges for the order to be advertised. The court also informs the Official Receiver of the making of the order immediately after it has been made (r 4.20). If the petition is dismissed, the court will draft the order and submit it to the petitioning creditor or his solicitor for engrossment. Once the order has been sealed by the court, the return of the deposit of £270 can be obtained.

6.4 Pre- and post-winding up

6.4.1 Restrictions If a company goes into liquidation, any disposition of its property (including payments made by it) after the date of the presentation of the petition is void (unless made with the consent of, or subsequently ratified by, the court) (s 127). Once a winding up petition has been presented, the court *may* stay any action or other legal process against the debtor or his property (s 126). The granting of a stay is discretionary. If the proceedings are pending in the High Court, that court may stay the proceedings. Otherwise application must be made to the court dealing with the winding up petition. Any attachment, distress or execution issued against the company is also void (s 128) and a creditor who, prior to the date of the presentation of the petition, issued an attachment or execution which remained incomplete at that date cannot retain the benefit of his action (s 183). A distraining creditor can retain the benefit of his distraint. Once a winding up order has been made or a provisional liquidator has been appointed, no creditor of the company may commence any action against the company without leave of the court (s 130). This rule does not affect the right of a creditor to the benefit of executions completed before the presentation of the winding up petition. Executions are complete when goods seized have been sold and proceeds held by the sheriff or bailiff for at least 14 days, when a charging order absolute has been obtained or when a debt garnisheed has been paid. A secured creditor is not affected by these provisions and can enforce his security though he cannot take any action in connection with any unsecured shortfall.

6.4.2 Provisional liquidator If it is necessary to protect the company's property prior to the hearing of the winding up petition, the court can, on the application of the company, the petitioner or a creditor, appoint the Official Receiver or some other fit person (ie an authorised insolvency practitioner) as provisional liquidator (s 135). The court will specify the powers which the provisional liquidator is to have (s 135(4) and r 4.26). A deposit for the costs of the provisional liquidator if he is the Official Receiver will be required from the party making the application (r 4.27). An application for the appointment of a provisional liquidator must be supported by an affidavit stating: why a provisional liquidator is thought necessary (eg, that the directors are dissipating the assets of the company); that the person proposed to be appointed is an authorised insolvency practitioner and is prepared to act; and whether the Official Receiver has been informed of the application (r 4.25). If the company is already the subject of an administration order or a company voluntary arrangement (see chapters 11 and 12) or is in voluntary liquidation or receivership, this must also be stated. The court will need persuading why the administrator, supervisor, (voluntary) liquidator or receiver cannot be left in charge of the company's assets until the hearing of the winding up petition.

6.4.3 Rescission Every court having jurisdiction in winding up proceedings may review, rescind or vary any order made by it (r 7.47). An application to rescind must normally be made within seven days, though the court will extend the time for applying in appropriate cases (*Re Virgo Systems Ltd* (1989) 5 BCC 833). If the proceedings have been transferred from one court to another after the making of the winding up order, the transferee court can also exercise this power. The court will not rescind an order simply because the company asks for it and the petitioning creditor or the general body of creditors also consent. The court has an obligation to look into all the circumstances before rescinding a winding up order.

6.4.4 Statement of affairs In all cases where a winding up order is made and later the appointment of a provisional liquidator, the directors or other officers of the company are obliged to submit a statement of affairs (s 131). The statement must be submitted to the Official Receiver within 21 days of the making of the winding up order or the appointment of a provisional liquidator (s 131(4)) or such longer time as the court or the Official Receiver may allow (s 131(5)). The statement must contain full particulars of the company's creditors, debts and other liabilities and of its assets together with such information as may be prescribed. Form 4.17 (in Sched 4 to the Rules) is the prescribed form for the statement of affairs. The Official Receiver is obliged to give to the persons obliged to provide a statement of affairs copies of this form (r 4.32(5)). The statement of affairs must be verified by an affidavit delivered together with a copy (s 131(2)). If the deponent cannot itself prepare a proper statement of affairs, the Official Receiver may employ someone at the expense of the company to assist or may authorise an allowance out of the company's assets towards the expense incurred by him in employing someone to assist in its preparation. The Official Receiver must receive an estimate from the bankrupt of the likely costs to be incurred and only a named person, approved by the Official Receiver can be authorised to do the work (r 4.37). If the person obliged to provide the statement of affairs fails without reasonable excuse to lodge a statement of affairs then he is liable to a fine (s 131(7)). The Official Receiver can require the former officers of the company to furnish accounts relating to three years prior to the winding up order and the court can order that accounts for earlier years be submitted also (r 4.39). The Official Receiver can also require the former officers to give further information explaining or amplifying anything contained in the statement of affairs or accounts (r 4.42).

6.4.5 Public examination The Official Receiver may make an application to the court for the public examination of the former officers (defined in s 133(1)(c)) to be held. The application must be accompanied by a report indicating that the proposed examinee falls within s 133. The Official Receiver *must* make an application for a public examination if requested to do so by half in value of the creditors or 75 per cent of the contributories. If the examinee fails to attend the public examination without reasonable excuse, he is guilty of contempt of court (s 134) but if he is unfit to undergo a public examination, he can make application to the court for the examination to be conducted in some other manner (r 4.25(4)). At the public examination, the Official Receiver, the liquidator, any creditor who has tendered a proof of debt or any contributory can ask questions and can with the approval of the court, appear by solicitor or counsel or authorise in writing another person to question the bankrupt on his behalf (r 4.21(5)). The examinee must take the oath and answer all the questions as the court may put or allow to be put. He may employ a solicitor or counsel at his own expense for the purpose of enabling him to explain or qualify any answers given (r 4.21(5)). The examinee is not entitled to refuse to answer questions on the ground that he may incriminate himself, but if criminal proceedings have been commenced against a director and the court is of the opinion that the continuation of the examination would be likely to prejudice a fair trial of those proceedings, the examination may be adjourned (r 4.21(5)(c)). A written record of the proceedings is taken and ultimately has to be signed by the examinee and verified by affidavit at a later date. This written record can be used as evidence against a director in any proceedings against him though not against third parties. The public examination may be adjourned from time to time either to a fixed date or generally (r 4.21(6)).

6.4.6 Private examination
The court may order any former officer of the company or any person thought to have information relating to the property of the company to attend court and to answer questions (s 236(11)). If the examinee does not attend he can be arrested and brought before the court (s 236(5)). If the evidence given by the examinee shows that he has property of the company, he can be ordered to deliver it up to the liquidator (s 237).

An order for a private examination will not be made against a person against whom the liquidator has already commenced or formed the intention of commencing proceedings unless only a protective writ has been issued. For the principles surrounding the granting of an order for private examination, see *Re Castle New Homes Ltd* [1979] 1 WLR 1075.

6.4.7 Appointment of liquidator
Unless or until someone else is appointed liquidator, the Official Receiver is the liquidator of the company. A liquidator can be appointed by a general meeting of the creditors by the court (where a liquidation follows on administration (s 140)) or by the Secretary of State (where the Official Receiver considers one appropriate). Only an authorised insolvency practitioner can act as a liquidator. To do so otherwise is an offence (s 389). Two or more liquidators can be appointed to act jointly. The Official Receiver must decide within 12 weeks after the making of the winding up order whether or not to summon a meeting of creditors and contributories for the purpose of choosing someone to be the liquidator (s 136(5)). If he decides that meetings should be called, those meetings must be held not more than four months from the date of the winding up order and 21 days' notice must be given to all creditors and contributories (r 4.56). Notice must also be given by advertisement in a local newspaper and the *London Gazette*. If the Official Receiver decides not to call a meeting of creditors but receives a request from a creditor supported by at least 25 per cent in value of all the other creditors, he must call a meeting (s 136(5)). That meeting must be held within three months (r 4.50(6)). In fixing the venue of the meetings, the Official Receiver must have regard to the convenience of those who are to attend and meetings must be held between 10 am and 4 pm on business days unless the court orders otherwise (r 4.60). The notices convening the meetings must also include a form of proxy to enable creditors and contributories who cannot attend the meetings to appoint someone else to attend on their behalf. Former officers and employees of the company can also be required by the Official Receiver to attend the meeting (r 4.58).

6.4.8 Rules governing meetings The following rules apply to all meetings of creditors and contributories. The Official Receiver acts as chairman at the first meeting and the liquidator at all other meetings. Resolutions are deemed to be passed on a majority in value of the creditors and contributories present personally or by proxy and vote in favour of it (r 4.63). There has to be a quorum present otherwise the meeting must be adjourned. The quorum is at least one creditor and in the case of the contributories meeting, two contributories, in person or by proxy. If the chairman by himself or with one creditor would constitute a quorum and the chairman is aware that other creditors intend to attend, the meeting must not commence until at least 15 minutes after the appointed time (r 12.4A(4)). If the meetings have to be adjourned, they must be adjourned for not more than 21 days. No creditor can vote at any creditors' meeting unless he has lodged proof of debt in the appropriate form and the claim has been admitted for the purpose of entitlement to vote (r 4.67) but the chairman can decide to allow a creditor to vote notwithstanding the absence of a proof if its absence was beyond the creditor's control (r 4.68). Creditors cannot vote if their debts are unliquidated nor if their debts are secured, though a partially secured creditor can value his security and vote for his unsecured shortfall. Contributories vote in accordance with the articles of association of the company (r 4.69). The chairman can decide to reject a proof for voting purposes but that decision is subject to appeal (r 4.70). If the chairman is in doubt as to the validity of a claim, he should mark the proof of debt accordingly and allow the creditor to vote subject to his vote being subsequently declared invalid if the objection is sustained (r 4.70(3)). If the validity of this particular proof had a material effect on the outcome of the meeting, the court may order a further meeting (r 4.70(4)). Where the chairman holds a proxy requiring him to vote for a particular resolution, he must propose that resolution if no one else does or unless he considers that there is good reason for not doing so (r 4.64).

A creditor may only vote in person or by a proxy. Only a sole trader or other individual can vote in person. All other creditors have to use proxies to give authority to someone to attend the meeting and vote on their behalf. A company can authorise a person to attend creditors' meetings and vote on its behalf by a resolution under s 375 of the Companies Act 1985. A copy of the authority must either be under the seal of the company or be certified as a true copy by a secretary or a director (r 8.7). There is no appeal against the decision of the chairman to declare invalid a proxy that has been lodged and so disentitle that creditors' representative from voting, but it is open to the creditor affected to apply to the court for the chairman's decision to be reversed and for a new meeting to be held. Forms of proxy must be sent out with notices summoning meetings. Only the prescribed form—Form 8.4—of proxy can be used. A proxy can either be a general proxy—allowing the proxy holder to use his discretion on voting—or a special proxy—requiring the proxy holder to vote for or against any specified resolution. The Official

Receiver can be appointed as proxy holder by a creditor. Proxies intended for use at a meeting must be lodged by the time stated in the notice summoning the meeting. No improper solicitation must be used in obtaining proxies or in procuring an appointment as trustee and if such improper solicitation has been used, no remuneration will be allowed to the person who has benefited by reason of such solicitation. A proxy holder may not vote in favour of a resolution which would place him in a position to receive any remuneration out of the estate unless the proxies are in the form of special proxies, provided that if the proxy holder himself has signed the proxy in his own favour he produces to the chairman written authorisation from the principal sufficient to show that he was authorised to sign (r 8.6(1A)).

6.4.9 Business at first meeting
The primary purpose of the first meeting is to appoint a liquidator. No resolution can be proposed which has at its object the appointment of the Official Receiver as liquidator (r 4.52(3)). The Official Receiver will remain the liquidator only if no other nominations are put forward and the Official Receiver does not ask the Secretary of State to appoint another person as liquidator. The meeting can also resolve to establish a liquidation committee (see also below). Unless a liquidation committee has been established, the meeting can specify the terms of the liquidator's remuneration. No person can be appointed as liquidator unless he is a qualified insolvency practitioner. Whoever is the chairman of the meeting must certify the appointment of the liquidator but cannot do so unless the person appointed has provided him with a written statement that he is a qualified insolvency practitioner and consents to act (r 4.100(2)). A liquidator's appointment is effective from the date the certificate of appointment is received from the Official Receiver. If the creditors and contributories nominate a different person to be liquidator, the creditors' choice prevails, though any creditor or contributory can apply to the court for someone else to be appointed (s 139).

6.4.10 Change of liquidator
For the liquidator to resign, he must call a meeting of creditors and give an account of his administration (r 4.108). A liquidator may only resign because of ill-health, his ceasing to be a qualified insolvency practitioner or because of some conflict of interest. If there is no quorum at the meeting of creditors to consider the liquidator's request to be allowed to resign, his resignation is deemed to have been accepted. Notice of the meeting must also be given to the Official Receiver and he must be informed of its outcome. During any vacancy of the post of liquidator such as that caused by the death of the liquidator, the Official Receiver becomes the liquidator (s 123). He must then decide whether or not to convene a further meeting of creditors having regard to the state of the administration of the liquidation. A liquidator other than the Official Receiver can be removed by resolution of creditors at a meeting duly summoned of which proper notice has been given (s 171). The court can remove a liquidator on the application

of an interested person. The Secretary of State can remove a liquidator, having given the liquidator notice of his intention to do so so that representations against his removal can be made (r 4.123).

6.4.11 The liquidation committee Creditors can resolve to establish a liquidation committee (s 141) but a committee cannot be established at any time when the Official Receiver is liquidator (s 141(4)). Any creditor other than a secured creditor is eligible to be a member of the committee provided that he has lodged a proof of debt and his proof of debt has not been disallowed (r 4.152(3)). A body corporate can be a member of the committee but can only act through a representative (r 4.152(5)). A creditors' committee must consist of at least three and not more than five members (r 4.152(1)). In the case of a solvent winding up, contributories can be members of the committee, up to three in number, and elected by the contributories at their meeting.

The role of the committee is primarily supervisory though it is also one of its functions to determine the liquidator's remuneration (r 4.127(3)). It can determine that the liquidator should be paid a percentage of the value of the assets realised or distributed or on a time basis. No resolution of the committee can override the general rule that where a liquidator has used improper solicitation to obtain proxies so as to procure his appointment as liquidator, no remuneration is allowable to him. The liquidator is under a duty to report to the committee all matters of concern to it with respect to the administration of the estate (r 4.155). The liquidator must send a report to every member of the committee from time to time (not less than once every six months or as and when directed by the committee, though not more often than once every two months) (r 4.162). The first meeting of the committee must take place within three months of its establishment and thereafter within 21 days of a request for a meeting by a member of a committee. The liquidator chairs the meeting of the committee (r 4.156).

The quorum for meetings of the committee is two (r 4.158). The liquidator can seek to obtain the agreement of the committee to a resolution by sending to every member a copy of the proposed resolution (r 4.167). In the absence of a request for a meeting to consider the resolution, the resolution is deemed to have been passed if and when the liquidator is notified in writing by a majority that they concur. A committee member may resign by notice to the liquidator and his membership is automatically terminated if he becomes bankrupt or is absent from three consecutive meetings (unless it is resolved that this rule should not apply at the third meeting) or if he ceased to be or is found never to have been a creditor (r 4.161). Vacancies of the committee need not be filled and if the majority of the remaining members agree, the liquidator can either appoint some other creditor to be a member of the committee if the majority of the remaining members agree or convene a meeting of creditors to appoint someone else. This applies equally to members of the committee appointed by the contributories. No member of the committee who is representative or associate nor anyone who has been a member of the committee within the last 12 months may enter into any transaction whereby he receives out of the liquidation any payment for services given or goods supplied or obtains any profit from the administration or acquires any asset (r 4.170) except with the leave of the court or with the prior sanction of the committee (r 4.170(3)). Members of the committee are entitled to receive their expenses for attending meetings but otherwise are not entitled to any payment out of the estate (r 4.169). Where there is no committee and the liquidator is other than the Official Receiver, the functions of the committee are performed by the Official Receiver on behalf of the Secretary of State. The liquidator can exercise certain powers only with the sanction of the liquidation committee. The matters requiring sanction are set out in Sched 4 to the Act. These powers include the right to carry on the business of the company, to prosecute or defend any legal actions and to compromise any dispute with one of the company's creditors or debtors.

CHAPTER 7

VOLUNTARY
LIQUIDATIONS

7.1 Members' voluntary liquidation

This chapter deals only with creditors' voluntary liquidations and not members' voluntary liquidations which come about when the shareholders of the company wish the company to be liquidated in circumstances other than its insolvency. Even though a company which is placed into members' voluntary liquidation is not insolvent, only a licensed insolvency practitioner can be the liquidator. If a company goes into members' voluntary liquidation and it subsequently transpires that the company is insolvent, then a meeting of creditors must be convened similar to a meeting under s 98 (see below) and to receive a statement of affairs (s 95) and to consider whether or not the (shareholders choice as) liquidator should continue in office.

7.2 Creditors' voluntary liquidation

7.2.1 Convening meetings When it appears to the directors that a company cannot continue to trade by reason of its insolvency, the directors can resolve to convene meetings of shareholders and creditors to consider and, if thought fit, to pass a resolution that the company be wound up. The shareholders' meeting must be convened in accordance with the memorandum and articles of association of the company and the Companies Act 1985. The creditors' meeting is governed by the Insolvency Act 1986 s 98. At least seven days' notice of the meeting must be given to creditors. The meeting must also be advertised in the *London Gazette* and two local newspapers. The creditors' meeting must be held not more than 14 days after the shareholders' meeting (s 98(1)) though both meetings are usually held on the same day. A list of creditors must be available for inspection at a place in the locality where the company traded or an insolvency practitioner must be named who can provide information to creditors on request (s 98(2)). The notice must state a time for the lodging of proxies to enable shareholders and creditors to vote at the meetings (if they cannot attend in person or they are not individuals). The latest time for the lodging of proxies must be not earlier than 12 noon on the business day before the meeting. A creditor is entitled to vote only if he is not a secured creditor, his claim is not unliquidated and he has lodged a claim (not necessarily in the form of a proof of debt) (r 4.67(2)) (though the chairman can excuse this last requirement if satisfied that failure was beyond the creditor's control (r 4.68)). The venue for the meeting must be fixed having regard to the convenience of those who are to attend and should be held between 10 am and 4 pm on a business day (r 4.69).

7.2.2 Purpose of meetings

The purpose of the meetings is to resolve to put the company into liquidation and to appoint a liquidator and a liquidation committee (ss 100 and 101). Shareholders and creditors may resolve a method of remuneration for the liquidator. If a company has already been placed in members' voluntary liquidation and it appears to the liquidator that all the creditors' debt will not be paid either in full or within 12 months of the liquidation commencing, he must call meetings of creditors in much the same way as meetings under s 98 (s 95).

7.2.3 The meetings

It is the duty of the directors to nominate one of their number to act as chairman of the meetings and to lay before the meetings a statement of affairs (s 99). The statement of affairs must be as up to date as possible and must be calculated to a date not more than 14 days before the date of the meeting. If the meeting has to be adjourned, then a new statement of affairs should be produced (r 4.34), though a report of the relevant matters since the statement of affairs will suffice (r 4.53B). The statement of affairs is that of the directors and must be delivered to the liquidator forthwith after the creditors' meeting. The cost of producing the statement of affairs and indeed of calling the meetings themselves can be borne out of the company's assets and, if payment for the preparation of a statement of affairs has been made, the meetings must be informed of who has been paid and how much.

The shareholders at their meeting not only resolve that the company should proceed to voluntary liquidation but also nominate someone to act as liquidator. If the creditors at their meeting make no fresh nomination, the shareholders' nominee as liquidator will be confirmed in office. If the creditors want to make an alternative nomination, they are free to do so and it is ultimately their wishes as to the choice of liquidator that will prevail. If there are more than two nominees for a liquidator from creditors, then there must be a series of votes with the nominee obtaining the least number of votes dropping out until there is a clear winner.

Voting is by reference to the value of creditors' claims. Creditors can attend either in person or by proxy and can lodge either a general proxy to enable the proxy holder to vote as he wishes or a special proxy requiring the proxy holder to vote in a particular way. There is a prescribed form of proxy in Sched 4 to the Rules: Form 8.5. If the chairman holds special proxies directing him to vote in a particular way, he must propose the resolution as directed by the special proxy unless he has good reason not to do so. In such a case, he must inform the proxy holder, subsequent to the meeting, of his reason (r 4.64).

For both the meetings of shareholders and creditors to be effective, there must be a quorum. A quorum is present in the case of a shareholders' meeting if there are two shareholders present (all the shareholders if there are less than two) and in the case of creditors' meetings if there is one creditor present. If no creditors are present in person but the chairman of the meeting knows in advance that certain creditors intend to attend the meeting but that they are not present at the time for the beginning of the meeting, he must not commence the meeting for 15 minutes to allow for the late-comers to arrive (r 12.4A).

7.2.4   Liquidator's duties after the meeting

The liquidator must advertise his appointment in a local newspaper (r 4.106) and also lodge a notice of his appointment with the Registrar of Companies. The liquidator can ask the directors to produce accounts and can provide for the cost of the preparation of these accounts out of the company's assets (rr 4.40 and 4.41). The liquidator is obliged to give all creditors within 28 days of the meeting a copy of the statement of affairs and a report of what took place at the meeting (r 4.49). Where a shareholders' meeting has been adjourned, the resolution to wind up takes effect from the date of the adjourned meeting (r 4.53A). Immediately the company is in liquidation, the directors' powers cease and only the liquidator has any power to act in the name of the company (s 103). If any vacancy arises in the post of liquidator because of the death, resignation or otherwise of the liquidator, the creditors may fill that vacancy (s 104).

The liquidator is under a duty to call annual meetings of shareholders and creditors to inform them of the progression of the liquidation (s 105) and must call a final meeting of shareholders and members to approve his account before the company can be dissolved (s 106). The liquidator may call meetings to ascertain the wishes of creditors whenever he thinks it necessary (r 4.54). He must convene a meeting if asked to do so by 10 per cent in value of the creditors (s 168). Such a meeting must be convened on 21 days' notice and must be held not later than 35 days after the request was made (r 4.57). All meetings of creditors subsequent to the appointment of the liquidator are chaired by the liquidator himself (r 4.56). Whenever a notice convening a meeting is sent out, proxy forms must also be issued.

7.2.5   Other matters

Most of the rules relating to the conduct of a creditors' voluntary liquidation are the same or similar to those applicable to compulsory liquidations. Creditors are not however required to lodge a formal proof of debt. It is sufficient for them to make a claim in any form, but the liquidator can require them to supply further particulars (r 4.76) or even an affidavit (r 4.77). The rules as to admission and rejection of creditors' claims are the same as for compulsory liquidation. Similarly, the rules for quantification of creditors' claims including the rights of secured creditors governed by rr 4.86 to 4.99 are the same as in compulsory liquidation. If the liquidator wishes to resign or creditors wish him to be removed, there are similar provisions as to those which apply in compulsory liquidations and are to be found in rr 4.108 to 4.123. The liquidator may have agreed at the s 98 meeting the method by which he is to be remunerated but the rules as to the remuneration of a liquidator are set out in rr 4.127 to 4.132 and are similar to those which apply in compulsory liquidations. Likewise the rule that a liquidator who uses improper solicitation in order to obtain appointment of a liquidator should not be entitled to any remuneration notwithstanding any vote of the liquidation committee to the contrary applies equally to voluntary liquidations as to compulsory liquidations (r 4.150).

In most voluntary liquidations the liquidator will be assisted by a liquidation committee. The rules regarding such committees are to be found in rr 4.151 to 4.172A and are similar to those applying to compulsory liquidation except that where there is no liquidation committee, the Secretary of State does not act as the committee whereas in compulsory liquidations he does. In the event that the liquidator does not have a liquidation committee, he must obtain those sanctions which he requires from the general body of creditors or the court.

CHAPTER 8

ALL LIQUIDATIONS

8.1 Liquidator's powers

8.1.1 Disclaimer The liquidator may disclaim any property of the company which is onerous (s 178). Onerous property is defined as any unprofitable contract and any other property which is unsaleable or may give rise to a liability to pay money or perform any other onerous act on the part of the company (s 178(3)). The liquidator may disclaim notwithstanding that he has endeavoured to sell the property in question. There is no right to disclaim a contract affecting land simply because that contract is not beneficial without disclaiming the property itself. In order to disclaim, the liquidator must give a notice in the prescribed form (Form 4.53 in Sched 4 to the Rules), file at court the notice and serve the same on the party affected. A liquidator does not need leave of the court to disclaim. There is no time limit within which the liquidator can disclaim unless he has been served with notice by the person interested in the property requiring him to make a decision within 28 days (s 178(5)). If the liquidator disclaims a lease, the court can vest the property in any person claiming an interest in that property, the guarantor of any liability in respect of the property or, in the case of a dwelling-house, in the occupant (s 181). Disclaimer operates so as to determine the rights, interests and liabilities of the company in respect of a disclaimed property. Disclaimer does not affect the rights and liabilities of third parties except in so far as is necessary in releasing the company from any liability (s 178(4)). Accordingly, a guarantor of a lease disclaimed by the liquidator is released from any further liability as from the date of disclaimer (*Stacey v Hill* [1901] 1 KB 660) unless the company was only an assignee of the lease (*Warnford Investments Ltd v Duckworth* [1979] 1 Ch 127).

8.1.2 Mutual credit and set off An account must be taken of what sum is due from the company to a person with whom there have been mutual credits, mutual debts or other mutual dealings (r 4.90). The sum due from one party must be set off against the sum due from the other and only the balance of the account is provable in the liquidation or is to be paid to the liquidator for the benefit of all creditors. For set off to be allowed, there must be obligations on both sides giving rise to pecuniary liabilities so that an account can be taken and the balance struck. If the obligation on one side is to deliver goods and on the other is to pay a sum of money, there can be no set off (see *Eberle's Hotel Co v Jonas* [1887] 18 QBD 459). In *Rolls Razor v Cox* [1967] 1 QBD 552, set off between sales commission and the value of goods in the possession of the salesman was allowed. Set off is mandatory and no contracting out is possible (*National Westminster Bank v Halesowen Presswork and Assemblies* [1972] AC 785). For set off to be successful, both liabilities must have arisen prior to the commencement of the liquidation even though one of the debts may not be immediately due and not enforceable until a time after the liquidation began. There can be no set off between joint debts and separate debts. Debts must be due in the same right. Set off will not be allowed where credit was given to the company by a creditor who had knowledge of the calling of a creditors' meeting under s 98 or of the presentation of a winding up petition (r 4.90(3)). If a creditor has to repay money to the liquidator (eg because of a preference) he cannot set off against the sum he is required to pay any sum due to him from the company (see *Elgood v Harris* [1896] 1 QB 419 and *Re A Debtor (No 82 of 1926)* [1927] 1 Ch 410). Right to set off may exist even though one of the debts is secured. Where a creditor has both a preferential and a non-preferential claim in a liquidation, the amount due from him to the company must be set off rateably (see *Re Unit 1 Windows Ltd* [1985] 1 WLR 1383). It may be possible to set off against a debt due from one party, a contingent liability of the other (see *Carreras Rothman Ltd v Freeman Matthews Treasurer* [1985] Ch 207, *Re Charge Card Services* [1986] 3 WLR 697 and *Re A Debtor (No 66 of 1955)* [1956] 1 WLR 226). A Crown department can set off against a debt due by it any debt owed by the company to another Crown department (*Re Cushla* [1973] 3 All ER 415 and *Re D H Curtis (Builders) Ltd* [1978] Ch 162).

8.1.3 General control of the liquidator There are many powers which the liquidator can exercise only with permission of a liquidation committee or, if there is no committee, with permission of the Secretary of State. Some powers can be exercised without sanction in a voluntary liquidation but only with sanction in a winding up by the court. These powers are set out in ss 165 and 166 (voluntary liquidation) and s 167 (winding up by the court) and Sched 4:

- carrying on the business of the company (in a winding up by the court);
- instituting or defending any legal actions (in a winding up by the court);
- compromising any claim of the company against a third party; and
- compromising any dispute with the company's creditors.

The liquidator may, without the permission of the liquidation committee, sell the company's property and borrow money on the security of the company's assets. If the liquidator does anything which requires permission but without obtaining that permission, his actions can be ratified if the committee is satisfied that he acted in a case of urgency and applied to the committee without undue delay (r 4.184(2)). The liquidator does not require the committee's sanction to employ a solicitor. He should, however, give notice of his actions to the liquidation committee. The liquidator has power to summon meetings of creditors so as to ascertain creditors' wishes (r 4.54). Creditors have the right to apply to the court for any decision of the liquidator to be reversed or modified if they are dissatisfied. The liquidator's remuneration is determined by the liquidation committee but if the liquidator is not satisfied with the decision of the committee, he can call a meeting of creditors to resolve otherwise (r 4.129). If still not satisfied, he can apply to the court (r 4.130). Similarly, creditors can apply to the court for the liquidator's remuneration to be reduced even though it has been approved by the liquidation committee (r 4.131). The liquidation committee can require the liquidator to insist that his solicitor's fees be taxed notwithstanding that he is of the opinion that they are reasonable (r 7.34(2)).

The liquidator is subject to control by the court on the application of any creditor or contributory. The liquidator is subject to control by the Department of Trade on the monetary aspects of his administration. The liquidator in a winding up by the court is required to pay all monies into the Insolvency Services Account at the Bank of England within 14 days of receipt of funds. In a voluntary liquidation he must pay all monies received by him and undistributed after six months into the Insolvency Services Account at the Bank of England. He is also obliged to send to the Secretary of State an account of all his receipts and payments every year. The court will not allow a liquidator in a winding up by the court (its officer) to retain or claim monies for distribution amongst the creditors when it would be inconsistent with natural justice to do so and something which an honest man would not do. This principle was first enunciated in *Re Condon, ex parte James* [1874] 9 Ch App 609 and was considered in *Re T H Knitwear (Wholesale) Ltd* (1988) 4 BCC 102.

8.1.4   Adjustment of prior transactions

The kind of matters liable to be set aside are transactions at an undervalue or preferences (ss 239 and 240). The liquidator has power to apply to the court for the reversal of certain transactions if they were to the disadvantage of the company and were carried out at a 'relevant time'. The relevant time is defined in s 240 in relation to transactions at an undervalue or a preference as being any time in the two years preceding the onset of insolvency but, in the case of preferences not benefiting a connected person, at any time in the period of six months prior to the onset of insolvency. Transactions cannot be set aside if the company was able to pay its debts at the time of the events or became unable to do so as a result. A company is deemed to be unable to pay its debts if it has failed to comply with a statutory demand served on it, or has allowed execution to go unsatisfied (s 123(1)) or if its liabilities (including contingent and prospective liabilities) exceed its assets at the time (s 123(2)).

Where a company entered into a transaction at an undervalue at a relevant time, the court can order the return of the benefit (s 241). For an order to be made, the court must be satisfied that the company had entered into a transaction. A positive act is required. The court has to fix the invalidity point (with no consideration to full value). It has been held that the invalidity point was above the level of nominal or insignificant consideration but below the level of equality (*Re Abbott (a bankrupt)* [1983] Ch 45). Where the company makes a preference at a relevant time, the recipient of a preference can be made to repay to the liquidator that which he received (s 241). The court must not make such an order unless it is satisfied that the company was influenced in deciding to make the transfer or payment to the recipient by a desire to prefer him (s 239(5)), but it is sufficient if only one of the motives in making the payment was a desire to prefer. (See *Re M C Bacon Ltd* (1989) *The Times*, 1 December for a discussion of 'desire' or 'intent' to prefer.) It is presumed in the case of a preference in favour of an associate that there was a desire to prefer (s 239(6)).

Where a creditor has, before the commencement of the winding up, issued execution against the goods or land of the company or attached any debt due to it, he cannot retain the benefit of his actions as against the liquidator unless execution or attachment was completed prior to the commencement of the winding up. All forms of distraint are subject to the rule that if they have taken place in the three months prior to the making of the winding up order, the proceeds of the distraint are 'charged' with the preferential debts (s 176(2)).

No lien or other right to possession of any books, papers or other records of the company is enforceable against the liquidator (s 246).

8.2 Debts and dividends

8.2.1 Types of creditor There are four classes of creditor—secured, preferential, unsecured and deferred. A secured creditor is not given any special priority by the Act or the Rules but can rely on his security. He may, with the agreement of the liquidator and leave of the court, at any time alter the value which he has, in his proof of debt, placed on his security, though if he petitioned for the winding up of the company or has voted in respect of his unsecured balance he may only revalue his security with leave of the court (r 4.95). If a secured creditor omits to disclose his security in his proof of debt, he must surrender it for the general benefit of creditors unless the court relieves him on the ground that omission was by mistake (r 4.96). A liquidator may redeem the security of the value placed on it by the creditor if he so wishes and a secured creditor has the right to call on the liquidator to elect whether or not to exercise this power (r 4.97).

Preferential debts are defined in s 386 and Sched 6 to the Act. They consist primarily of taxes such as PAYE, VAT, and social security contributions. Amounts due to employees for wages for the four months prior to the making of the winding up order or resolution to wind up but not exceeding £800 for each employee are also preferential, together with all arrears of holiday pay. If monies have been advanced by a third party to pay wages and holiday pay which otherwise would have been preferential debts, then the person who advanced the money becomes a preferential creditor for the amount advanced.

Unsecured creditors are the ordinary debts of the company which are neither secured nor preferential.

8.2.2   Provable debts   All claims by creditors against the company are provable in the liquidation whether they are present or future, certain or contingent, ascertained or sounding only in damages (r 12.3). Even unliquidated damages of tort are provable debts.

8.2.3   Proofs of debt   Every person claiming to be a creditor in a winding up by the court must submit his claim in writing to the Official Receiver or the liquidator—this is called proving his debt. In voluntary liquidations, formal proofs of debt are not usually required—a claim in any form is sufficient but the liquidator can call for a formal proof of debt to be submitted. A proof of debt must be in the prescribed form (Form 4.25 in Sched 4 to the Rules) or a substantially similar form. Proofs of debt forms must be sent out by the Official Receiver or liquidator to every creditor who is known to him or identified in the statement of affairs. The liquidator may require a proof of debt to be verified by affidavit in Form 4.26. Such an affidavit can be sworn by the creditor before his own solicitor (r 7.57). A proof of debt must contain details of the creditor's name and address, the amount owing, the date of the liquidation, whether interest and VAT is included, whether any part of the debt is preferential, how the debt was incurred and particulars of any security held and if so its value (r 4.75). If the debt was incurred in a foreign currency, the sterling equivalent must be stated as at the date of the liquidation. There is no time limit for the submission of proofs of debt but a creditor who has not proved his debt cannot benefit from any distribution nor can he vote at any meeting of creditors until proof has been lodged. Before declaring a dividend, the liquidator must give notice of his intention to do so to all creditors of whom he is aware and who have not proved their debts (r 11.2(1)). The notice must specify the last date for proving which must be not less than 21 days after the date of the notice and must state the liquidator's intention to declare a dividend. The liquidator must examine every proof of debt and admit it wholly or in part for dividend. If he rejects it, he must give his reasons in writing and inform the creditor concerned (r 4.82). The liquidator cannot declare a dividend until he has examined every proof of debt. Acceptance of a proof of debt for voting purposes at the first meeting is not the same as acceptance by the liquidator of a proof for dividend and the liquidator is not bound by the earlier decision of the Official Receiver. If a creditor is dissatisfied at the decision of the liquidator, the court may reverse that decision. No application to the court to vary the liquidator's decision will be entertained unless it is made within 21 days from the date of service by the liquidator of the notice of rejection with reasons (r 4.93(1)). This time limit, as with all other time limits, is extendable by the court.

8.2.4 Interest

When a debt proved in a liquidation bears interest (contractual or statutory), the proof of debt can include interest up to the date of the liquidation (r 4.93(1)). If the debt does not include the right to interest, interest can nonetheless be claimed up to the date of liquidation. If the debt arose by virtue of a written instrument and in respect of a debt payable at a certain time, then at the judgment rate or otherwise after demand for payment has been made stating that interest will be charged thereafter (at a rate not exceeding judgment rate) (r 4.93(3) and (4)). Interest on preferential debts would not appear also to be preferential. If there is a surplus remaining after paying all proved debts (including interest on them up to the date of liquidation) it will then be applied to the payment of interest on all proved debts *pari passu* at the greater of contractual or judgment rate.

8.2.5 VAT

A creditor whose claim includes an element of VAT can either prove for the whole amount of the claim (and pay to HM Customs and Excise the VAT element irrespective of whether or not he receives any dividend) or prove for the amount of his claim net of VAT and reclaim the VAT (Finance Act 1983 s 22(5)). No formalities are required to reclaim the VAT element of the debt owed by the bankrupt—the creditor is automatically entitled to VAT bad debt relief once he has written off the debt in his books and the debt is more than 6 months old.

8.2.6 Dividends

The liquidator must give notice of a dividend to all creditors who proved their debts. The notice must include details of the amounts realised from the sale of assets, payments made by the liquidator in his administration, the total amount distributed, the rate of dividend and whether any further dividends are to be expected. The liquidator must not, except with the leave of the court, proceed to declare a dividend where there is pending an application to vary a decision of his on a proof of debt. If the liquidator is unable to declare any or any further dividend, he must give notice to this effect to creditors. A creditor who has failed to lodge his proof of debt before an interim dividend was declared is not entitled to disturb that interim distribution but is entitled to receive a payment in priority to other creditors from further funds as available (r 4.182). The liquidator cannot be sued for a dividend but if he refuses to pay a dividend the court may order him to pay it together with, out of his own funds, interest at judgment rate and costs (r 4.182(3)). When the liquidator is ready to close his administration, he must give notice to the creditors of his intention to declare a final dividend or that no further dividend will be declared (r 4.186(1)). The notice must require any remaining claims to be established by a certain date: if they are not, they can be ignored by the liquidator (r 4.186(2) and (3)).

CHAPTER 9

RECEIVERSHIPS

9.1 Nature of receivership

There are three kinds of receivership—under the Law of Property Act 1925 in respect of a property, by the court and by a debenture holder under a floating charge debenture. Court appointed receivers are rare. If a receiver is appointed under a floating charge debenture, he is called an administrative receiver. All that appears subsequently in this chapter relates to administrative receiverships.

9.2 Appointment of receiver

The appointment of a receiver is of no effect unless it is accepted by the receiver before the end of the next business day (s 33). Acceptance must be in writing or confirmed in writing within seven days (r 3.1). The receiver can apply to the court for directions in relation to any matter arising in connection with the performance of his functions (s 35). The court can fix the receiver's remuneration if asked to so do by the liquidator of the company (s 36). The receiver must make it clear and every invoice, order or business letter issued by him must contain a statement that a receiver or manager has been appointed (s 39).

9.3 Liability of receiver

A receiver is personally liable on any contract entered into by him and even in relation to any contract of employment adopted by him, though he is entitled to indemnity out of the assets of the company (s 37). The receiver is deemed to be the agent of the company (unless the company goes into liquidation (s 34)).

9.4 Priority of debts in receivership

If an asset is subject to a fixed charge, the receiver need have regard to no debts in priority to those owed to the fixed charge holder. If assets are subject only to a floating charge, then the receiver must ensure that the preferential creditors of the company are paid in full before the debenture holder receives any payment. Preferential creditors are defined in Sched 6 of the Act. If there is a surplus from the sale of a fixed charge asset after paying off the amount due to the chargee, the surplus must not be used for the payment of preferential creditors but handed on to any liquidator subsequently appointed (*Re G L Saunders Ltd* [1986] 1 WLR 215).

Though a debenture states that it includes a fixed charge on book debts, it usually can only take effect as a floating charge if the debenture holder is not the company's bankers or has no control over the company's banking (*Re Brightlife* [1987] 2 WLR 197).

9.5   Powers of a receiver

The powers confirmed on a receiver are set out in Sched 1 to the Act and include the right to take or defend proceedings in the company's name, sell the company's assets, borrow money, appoint solicitors, use the company seal, carry on business and even petition for the winding up of the company. The receiver has power to apply to the court to allow the disposal of an asset subject to a fixed charge as if that asset were not subject to such security. This is in order to prevent a creditor owed more than the value of his security preventing beneficial realisation of the company's assets (s 43 and r 3.31).

An English receiver's powers extend to assets in Scotland and vice versa (s 72).

9.6   Duties of a receiver

The receiver is under an obligation to notify the company and advertise notice of his appointment and within 28 days to send a similar notice to all creditors of the company (s 46(1)). Every receiver or manager of a company's property (other than an administrative receiver) must deliver to the Registrar of Companies an account of his receipts and payments every 12 months (s 38). An administrative receiver must report to creditors within three months after his appointment and send to the Registrar of Companies and to all creditors a report on the events leading up to his appointment, details of what property is being disposed by him, the amount owed to the debenture holders and to preferential creditors and the amount, if any, likely to be available for ordinary creditors (s 48(1)). He must lay a copy of his report before a meeting of the company's ordinary creditors within the same timescale (s 48(2)).

The meeting of creditors can decide to establish a committee 'to assist the receiver'. The committee can require the receiver to attend meetings and to provide it with information (s 49). The court can dispense with the meeting under s 48 but creditors must be told of the receiver's application for dispensation (r 3.8). The rules governing the conduct of the creditors' meeting in a receivership are contained in rr 3.9–3.15. The functions of the creditors' committee are to assist the receiver and to act as agreed with him (r 3.18). The usual rules as to meetings of the committee and resolutions passed by it apply (see 7.4).

9.7 Statement of affairs

After an administrative receiver has been appointed, the directors of the company are under an obligation to submit a statement of affairs (s 47). The statement should be in Form 3.2 in Sched 4 to the Rules and must be verified by affidavit (r 3.4). The court can order limited disclosure of the information contained in the statement of affairs or even release the directors from the obligation to submit such a statement (rr 3.5 and 3.6).

9.8 VAT

No formalities are required to reclaim the VAT element of the debt owed by the bankrupt—the creditor is automatically entitled to VAT bad debt relief once he has written off the debt in his books and the debt is more than 6 months old.

COMPANY VOLUNTARY ARRANGEMENTS

10.1 Nature of a company voluntary arrangement (CVA)

A CVA is an agreement between a company and its shareholders and creditors. There is little court involvement. It is only necessary for copies of certain documents to be lodged at court so as to be available for public inspection. Only an authorised insolvency practitioner may be the nominee and supervisor in a CVA. A CVA can be proposed even after a company has gone into administration or liquidation.

The object of a CVA can either be a moratorium (a delay of payment until a certain event happens or payment by instalments) or the payment of less than 100p in the pound in full settlement.

10.2 The proposal

The directors of a company, the liquidator or administrator (if the company is in administration) can make a proposal for a CVA (s 1). The proposal must contain an explanation why a CVA is desirable and why the company's creditors might be expected to agree to it. The proposal must set out details of the company's assets and liabilities, how it is proposed to deal with secured and preferential creditors and creditors who are connected with the company, whether there are any circumstances that might give rise to an adjustment of prior transactions, what costs were involved in the CVA, what duties the supervisor will undertake and so on (r 1.3). For a precedent of a set of proposals for a CVA, see Appendix 2, form 2.

If it is the directors who are putting forward the proposal, they must select an authorised insolvency practitioner to act as nominee. It is the nominee's duty to report to the creditors (and the court) on the directors' proposals (r 1.7). The proposers of the proposal must give to the nominee a statement of affairs relating to the company (r 1.5) and all these documents must be lodged in court. If the nominee is of the opinion that there is some prospect of the CVA being approved, he will state that in his opinion a meeting of the shareholders and creditors of the company should be convened to consider the proposal (r 1.9).

10.3   Meetings of shareholders and creditors

For a CVA to be approved, shareholders and creditors must give their approval. The shareholders' meeting must be held on the same day but after the creditors' meeting. The meetings should be arranged for the convenience of those who are to attend (r 1.13). The rules as to the conduct of the meeting are contained in rr 1.14 to 1.16. For a CVA to be approved, there has to be a 75 per cent majority in favour of it. The majority is calculated by reference to the value of the creditors' claims of those creditors present in person or by proxy and voting at the meeting. Shareholders' approval is given by a simple majority (r 1.20). However, if more than half in value of those voting, excluding connective creditors, are against the proposal, it is not carried (r 1.19(4)). If it is not possible to obtain agreement to the proposal at the meeting of creditors, the meeting can be adjourned for a further try (r 1.21), but the adjournment must be for not more than 14 days. Shareholders and creditors may approve the CVA with or without modifications. If a company is prepared to accept the modifications proposed to it, the CVA takes effect as if those modifications were proposed by the company.

If any shareholder or creditor feels that the meetings have not been conducted in accordance with the rules or that the interests of a shareholder or member have been unfairly prejudiced by the CVA, he may apply to the court for revocation or suspension of the CVA (s 6). The court can order further meetings to be held (r 1.25).

10.4   Approval and implementation

An approved CVA binds every person who was given notice of, and was entitled to vote at, the meeting to consider the proposal whether or not he was actually present at that meeting. If the company is in administration or liquidation, the court may stay the proceedings and give directions with regard to the proceedings as are appropriate for facilitating the implementation of the CVA (s 5(3)). The winding up of the company is, however, not rescinded or reversed but simply stayed. The person whose function it is to carry out the CVA is the supervisor. He may apply to the court for directions in relation to any matters arising in the CVA and indeed may apply to the court for the company to be wound up or for an administration order to be made (s 7). Once a CVA is approved, the directors (or the administrator or liquidator as the case may be) must do everything that is required for putting the supervisor into possession of the assets included in the arrangement (r 1.23). The nominee is under an obligation to report the outcome of the meeting to the court and all the shareholders and creditors (r 1.24). Once the CVA is approved, no creditor who has been given notice of the creditors' meeting can take any action against the company in relation to his debt. This applies whether or not the creditor concerned attended the meeting or voted for or against the proposal.

10.5   Supervisor's duties

The supervisor has an obligation to keep accounts and records of his dealings and to prepare an account of all his receipts and payments not less than once every 12 months and send it to the court, the Registrar of Companies, shareholders and creditors (r 1.26). The supervisor must also produce to the Secretary of State his records and accounts if so requested (r 1.27). Not more than 28 days after the final completion of the CVA the supervisor must send to all shareholders and creditors a notice that the CVA has been fully implemented, and lodge a copy with the court (r 1.29).

ADMINISTRATIONS

11.1 Nature of administration

Administrations were introduced into the insolvency legislation with the object of promoting the rehabilitation of companies that had become insolvent (akin to chapter 11 of the US Bankruptcy Code). The purposes for which an administration order can be made are (s 8(3)):

- the survival of the company in whole or in part as a going concern;
- the approval of a voluntary arrangement;
- the sanctioning of a scheme under the Companies Act s 425; or
- a more advantageous realisation of the company's assets than would be the case in a winding up.

The court can make an administration order only if it is satisfied that the company is insolvent and that one of the purposes set out above would be likely to be achieved (s 8).

11.2 Application for an administration order (s 9)

An application for an administration order is made by petition either by the company, all the company's directors, creditors or the supervisor. The petition should be in Form 2.1 in Sched 4 to the Rules and must be supported by an affidavit (rr 2.1 and 3) together with the proposed administrator's report where available (r 2.2). The petition is presented to the court having jurisdiction to wind up the company, that is, the county court for the area where the company's registered office is situated if the share capital of the company is less than £120,000, or the High Court (be it in London or one of the eight provincial district registries). The petition must be served on the company, anyone entitled to appoint an administrative receiver, the administrative receiver if one has been appointed and the proposed administrator (r 2.6). The effect of an application for an administration order is that no steps can be taken in legal actions or executions against the company or its property except with leave of the court and no steps can be taken to enforce any security over the company's property while the application is pending, again except with leave of the court (s 10). Also, the company may not resolve to wind up while the application is pending. The court has power to make an interim order once an application has been lodged (s 9(4)). The court must not make an administration order if an administrative receiver has been appointed unless the appointer consents (s 9(3)).

On the hearing of the application, anyone entitled to appoint an administrative receiver may appear together with the petitioner of the company itself. In addition, with leave of the court, any other person who appears to have an interest may appear (r 2.9). It is the court which appoints the administrator (s 13), though the administrator is nominated by the applicant for the order. The administration order must specify the one or more purposes set out in s 8(3) which the administration order is intended to achieve. The form of order is Form 2.4 in Sched 4 to the Rules. Once an administration order is made, any petition for the winding up of the company is dismissed automatically and any administrative receiver must vacate office. Also, no resolution for the voluntary winding up of the company may be passed, no administrative receiver may be appointed and no steps may be taken in any legal proceedings against the company or for enforcement of any security over the company's assets except with leave of the court (s 11).

11.3 Powers of the administrator

The powers of the administrator are set out in Sched 1 to the Act. These powers are the same as for an administrative receiver and include the power to sell the company's property, to bring or defend proceedings in the company's name etc. However, no sale of the company's property can be effected by an administrator until he has put proposals to the creditors and a creditors' meeting has been held, unless the matter is one of urgency. The administrator can apply for directions at any time during his administration (s 14(3)).

11.4 Power to deal with charged property

An administrator may dispose of any charged property as if the property were not subject to any security, if the court is satisfied that the disposal of that property would be likely to promote one or more of the purposes specified in the administration order (s 15(1) and (2)). Where property is disposed of under s 15(1), the holder of this security has the same priority in respect of the proceeds of sale as he had over the property disposed of. It is a condition of the court granting an order under s 15(1) that the net proceeds of sale and, where the proceeds of sale are less than the amount which would have been realised on a sale in the open market, the sums required to make good the deficiency be paid towards discharging the sums due to the secured creditor. Section 15 applies equally to goods the subject of hire purchase agreements and goods the subject of retention of title claims. Rule 2.51 sets out the procedure for making the application.

11.5 Summoning creditors' meetings

The administrator must convene a meeting of creditors if requested to do so by 10 per cent in value of the creditors or if directed to do so by the court (s 17(3)). An administrator must also convene a meeting of creditors to consider his proposals under s 23—see below.

11.6 Discharge or variation of the order

The administrator may at any time apply to the court for the administration order to be discharged or varied (s 18(1)). He must make an application for the order to be discharged or varied if it appears to him that the purpose or each of the purposes specified in the order has been achieved or is incapable of achievement or if he is required to do so by a meeting of the company's creditors (s 18(2)). If an administration order is discharged, the administrator will be released from all liability in respect of his conduct only if the court so orders (s 20). Where a winding up order is made immediately on the discharge of an administration order, the court may appoint as liquidator the person who had been the administrator (s 140) but only after that person has informed the creditors of his intention to ask the court to appoint him liquidator (after discharge of the administration order) and after he has reported to the court on the response received from the creditors.

11.7 Investigation by administrator

The directors are under a duty (under s 22) to submit to the administrator a statement of affairs relating to the company, verified by affidavit (r 2.1(2). Limited disclosure or even release from the obligation to submit a statement of affairs may be ordered by the court (r 2.1(3) and (4)) or allowed by the administrator (s 22(5)). The administrator is under a duty to report to the DTI any conduct of the officers of the company which might merit their disqualification from acting as directors.

11.8 Administrator's proposals (s 23)

The administrator is under a duty to lay before a meeting of creditors, within three months of his appointment, his proposals. He must serve copies on all shareholders and advertise. Within the proposal must be a statement setting out details of his appointment or the purpose for which it was made, a copy of the statement of affairs and such other information as would be necessary to enable creditors to decide whether or not to vote for the adoption of the proposal (r 2.1(6)). At the meeting, creditors will decide whether to approve the administrator's proposals. The administrator must report the outcome of the meeting to the court and if the report states that the meeting has declined to approve the administrator's proposals, the court may discharge the administration order (s 24(5)). The rules as to the conduct of the meeting are set out in r 2.1(8) to 2.2(5) and are the usual rules that apply to all meetings of creditors under the insolvency legislation. Retention of title claimants must deduct the value of their rights when voting (r 2.2(6)). Creditors for hire purchase arrears can vote as ordinary creditors (r 2.2(7)). Where the administrator's proposals have been approved and the administrator proposes to make revisions to those proposals, he must inform all creditors of his proposed revisions and convene a further meeting of creditors on not less than 14 days' notice (s 25).

11.9   Creditors' committee

Where a meeting of creditors has been convened under s 23 and has approved the administrator's proposals, the meeting may, if it thinks fit, establish a creditors' committee (s 26(1)). The functions of the committee are to assist the administrator and to act in relation to him in such a manner as may be agreed from time to time (r 2.3(4)).

11.10   Protection of creditors and shareholders

At any time when an administration order is in force, a creditor or shareholder may apply to the court for an order on the grounds that his interests have been unfairly prejudiced or that any act or omission of the administrator would be prejudicial to his interests (s 27(1)). On such an application the court can make an order regulating the future management by the administrator, requiring the summoning of a meeting of creditors or even discharging the administration order (s 27(4)).

11.11   Remuneration of administrator

The administrator's remuneration is fixed either by the creditors' committee or, if there is no committee, by a meeting of creditors or, failing that, by the court. If the administrator is not satisfied with the fixing of his remuneration, he may apply to the court (rr 2.47 and 2.50). The administrator's remuneration can be fixed either by reference to the time spent by him or as a percentage of the value of the assets involved.

11.12   Duty of administrator to provide information

The administrator is under a duty within two months after the end of each six-month period after the date of his appointment to provide to the court, the Registrar of Companies and the creditors' committee an account of all his receipts and payments. This information must also be supplied within two months after the administrator has ceased to act.

11.13   VAT

No formalities are required to reclaim the VAT element of the debt owed by the bankrupt—the creditor is automatically entitled to VAT bad debt relief once he has written off the debt in his books and the debt is more than 6 months old.

COUNTY COURT AREAS AND BANKRUPTCY COURTS AND ALTERNATIVE FULL-TIME COURTS

County court	Court with bankruptcy jurisdiction	Nearest full-time court
Aberdare	Aberdare	Cardiff
Aberystwyth	Aberystwyth	Cardiff
Accrington	Blackburn	
Aldershot and Farnham	Guildford	
Alfreton	Derby	
Alnwick	Newcastle	
Altrincham	Manchester	
Amersham	Aylesbury	
Ammanford	Carmarthen	
Andover	Salisbury	
Ashford	Canterbury	
Axminster and Chard	Exeter	
Aylesbury	Aylesbury	Luton
Banbury	Banbury	Gloucester or Luton
Bangor	Bangor	Birkenhead or Chester
Bargoed	Blackwood	
Barnet	High Court	
Barnsley	Barnsley	Sheffield
Barnstaple	Barnstaple	Exeter
Barrow in Furness	Barrow in Furness	Blackpool
Barry	Cardiff	
Basingstoke	Reading	

County court	Court with bankruptcy jurisdiction	Nearest full-time court
Bath	Bath	Bristol
Bedford	Bedford	Luton
Berwick on Tweed	Newcastle	
Beverley	Kingston upon Hull	
Birkenhead	Birkenhead	
Birmingham	Birmingham	
Bishop Auckland	Durham	
Bishop's Stortford	Hertford	
Blackburn	Blackburn	Preston
Blackpool	Blackpool	
Blackwood	Blackwood	Cardiff
Blyth	Newcastle	
Bodmin	Truro	
Bolton	Bolton	
Boston	Boston	Nottingham
Bournemouth	Bournemouth	
Bow	High Court	
Bradford	Bradford	
Braintree	Chelmsford	
Brecknock	Merthyr Tydfil	
Brentford	High Court	
Brentwood	Southend	
Bridgend	Bridgend	Cardiff
Bridgwater	Bridgwater	Bristol
Bridlington	Scarborough	
Brighton	Brighton	
Bristol	Bristol	
Bromley	Croydon	
Burnley	Burnley	Bolton or Preston
Burton upon Trent	Burton upon Trent	Derby, Leicester or Nottingham
Bury	Bolton	
Bury St Edmunds	Bury St Edmunds	Cambridge
Buxton	Stockport	
Caernarvon	Bangor	
Caerphilly	Pontypridd	
Cambourne and Redruth	Truro	
Cambridge	Cambridge	
Canterbury	Canterbury	Croydon or High Court
Cardiff	Cardiff	
Cardigan	Carmarthen	

County court	Court with bankruptcy jurisdiction	Nearest full-time court
Carlisle	Carlisle	Blackpool or Preston
Carmarthen	Carmarthen	Cardiff
Central London	Central London	
Chelmsford	Chelmsford	Southend or High Court
Cheltenham	Cheltenham	Gloucester
Chepstow	Newport (Gwent)	
Chester	Chester	Birkenhead
Chesterfield	Chesterfield	Sheffield
Chichester	Brighton	
Chippenham	Bath	
Chorley	Preston	
Clerkenwell	High Court	
Colchester and Clacton	Colchester	Southend
Consett	Newcastle	
Conwy and Colwyn	Bangor	
Corby	Northampton	
Coventry	Coventry	Birmingham
Crewe	Crewe	Chester or Stoke
Croydon	Croydon	
Darlington	Darlington	Teeside
Dartford	Medway	
Derby	Derby	Nottingham
Dewsbury	Dewsbury	Leeds
Doncaster	Doncaster	Sheffield
Dover	Canterbury	
Dudley	Dudley	Birmingham
Durham	Durham	Newcastle
Eastbourne	Eastbourne	Brighton
East Grinstead	Tunbridge Wells	
Edmonton	High Court	
Ellesmere Port	Birkenhead	
Epsom	Croydon	
Evesham	Worcester	
Exeter	Exeter	
Folkestone	Canterbury	
Gainsborough	Lincoln	
Gateshead	Newcastle	
Gloucester	Gloucester	
Goole	Wakefield	
Grantham	Lincoln	
Gravesend	Medway	

County court	Court with bankruptcy jurisdiction	Nearest full-time court
Grays Thurrock	Southend	
Great Grimsby	Great Grimsby	Hull
Great Malvern	Worcester	
Great Yarmouth	Great Yarmouth	Norwich
Guildford	Guildford	Croydon
Halifax	Halifax	Leeds
Harlow	Hertford	
Harrogate	Harrogate	Leeds
Hartlepool	Stockton on Tees	
Hastings	Hastings	Brighton
Haverfordwest	Haverfordwest	Cardiff
Haywards Heath	Brighton	
Hemel Hempstead	St Albans	
Hereford	Hereford	Gloucester
Hertford	Hertford	Luton
Hexham	Newcastle	
High Wycombe	Aylesbury	
Hitchin	Luton	
Holywell	Rhyl	
Horsham	Brighton	
Huddersfield	Huddersfield	Leeds
Huntingdon	Peterborough	
Ilford	Romford	
Ilkeston	Derby	
Ipswich	Ipswich	Norwich or Southend
Keighley	Bradford	
Kendal	Kendal	Blackpool or Preston
Kettering	Northampton	
Kidderminster	Kidderminster	Birmingham
Kings Lynn	Kings Lynn	Cambridge or Norwich
Kingston upon Hull	Kingston upon Hull	
Kingston upon Thames	Kingston upon Thames	
Lambeth	High Court	
Lampeter	Carmarthen	
Lancaster	Lancaster	Blackpool or Preston
Launceston	Plymouth	
Leeds	Leeds	
Leicester	Leicester	
Leigh	Wigan	
Lewes	Brighton	

County court	Court with bankruptcy jurisdiction	Nearest full-time court
Lichfield	Walsall	
Lincoln	Lincoln	Nottingham
Liverpool	Liverpool	
Llandrindod Wells	Welshpool and Newtown	
Llanelli	Swansea	
Llangefni	Bangor	
Loughborough	Leicester	
Lowestoft	Great Yarmouth	
Ludlow	Hereford	
Luton	Luton	
Macclesfield	Macclesfield	Manchester or Stoke
Maidstone	Maidstone	Croydon or High Court
Maldon	Chelmsford	
Malton	York	
Manchester	Manchester	
Mansfield	Nottingham	
Market Drayton	Shrewsbury	
Marylebone	High Court	
Matlock	Derby	
Mayor and City of London	High Court	
Medway	Medway	Croydon or High Court
Melton Mowbray	Leicester	
Merthyr Tydfil	Merthyr Tydfil	Cardiff
Milton Keynes	Northampton	Luton
Mold	Chester	
Monmouth	Newport (Gwent)	
Morpeth	Newcastle	
Neath and Port Talbot	Neath	Cardiff
Nelson	Burnley	
Newark	Nottingham	
Newbury	Newbury	Reading
Newcastle upon Tyne	Newcastle	
Newport (IOW)	Newport (IOW)	Portsmouth or Southampton
Newport (Gwent)	Newport (Gwent)	Cardiff
Newton Abbot	Torquay	
Northallerton	Darlington	
Northampton	Northampton	Luton
North Shields	Newcastle	

County court	Court with bankruptcy jurisdiction	Nearest full-time court
Northwich	Crewe	
Norwich	Norwich	
Nottingham	Nottingham	
Nuneaton	Coventry	
Oldham	Oldham	
Oswestry	Wrexham	
Otley	Harrogate	
Oxford	Oxford	Reading
Penrith	Carlisle	
Penzance	Truro	
Peterborough	Peterborough	Cambridge
Plymouth	Plymouth	
Pontefract	Wakefield	
Pontypool	Newport (Gwent)	
Pontypridd	Pontypridd	Cardiff
Poole	Bournemouth	
Portmadoc	Portmadoc	Birkenhead, Chester or Stoke
Portsmouth	Portsmouth	
Preston	Preston	
Rawtenstall	Burnley	
Reading	Reading	
Redditch	Birmingham	
Reigate	Croydon	
Rhyl	Rhyl	Birkenhead or Chester
Rochdale	Rochdale	Manchester or Oldham
Romford	Romford	
Rotherham	Sheffield	
Rugby	Coventry	
Runcorn	Warrington	
St Albans	St Albans	Luton
St Austell	Truro	
St Helens	Liverpool	
Salford	Salford	
Salisbury	Salisbury	Bournemouth or Southampton
Scarborough	Scarborough	Hull, Teeside or York
Scunthorpe	Scunthorpe	Hull or Sheffield
Sevenoaks	Tunbridge Wells	
Shaftesbury	Salisbury	
Sheerness	Medway	

County court	Court with bankruptcy jurisdiction	Nearest full-time court
Sheffield	Sheffield	
Shoreditch	High Court	
Shrewsbury	Shrewsbury	Stoke
Sittingbourne	Medway	
Skegness and Spilsby	Boston	
Skipton	Bradford	
Sleaford	Boston	
Slough	Slough	
Southampton	Southampton	
Southend	Southend	
Southport	Liverpool	
South Shields	Sunderland	
Spalding	Peterborough	
Stafford	Stafford	Stoke
Staines	Slough	
Stockport	Stockport	Manchester
Stockton on Tees	Stockton on Tees	Teeside
Stoke on Trent	Stoke on Trent	
Stourbridge	Stourbridge	Birmingham
Stratford upon Avon	Warwick	
Stroud	Gloucester	
Sudbury	Colchester	
Sunderland	Sunderland	Newcastle
Swansea	Swansea	Cardiff
Swindon	Swindon	Gloucester or Reading
Tameside	Tameside	Manchester
Tamworth	Birmingham	
Taunton	Taunton	Bristol or Exeter
Teeside	Teeside	
Telford	Shrewsbury	
Thanet	Canterbury	
Thorne	Doncaster	
Todmorden	Halifax	
Torquay	Torquay	Exeter
Trowbridge	Bath	
Truro	Truro	Plymouth
Tunbridge Wells	Tunbridge Wells	Croydon
Uxbridge	Slough	
Wakefield	Wakefield	Leeds
Walsall	Walsall	

County court	Court with bankruptcy jurisdiction	Nearest full-time court
Wandsworth	High Court	
Warrington	Warrington	Chester, Liverpool or Manchester
Warwick	Warwick	Birmingham
Watford	St Albans	
Wellingborough	Northampton	
Welshpool and Newtown	Welshpool and Newtown	Chester or Stoke
West Bromwich	West Bromwich	Birmingham
West London	High Court	
Weston super Mare	Bristol	
Weymouth	Weymouth	Bournemouth
Whitby	Scarborough	
Whitehaven	Workington	
Wigan	Wigan	Bolton, Manchester or Preston
Willesden	High Court	
Winchester	Winchester	Southampton
Wisbech	Kings Lynn	
Wolverhampton	Wolverhampton	
Woolwich	Croydon	
Worcester	Worcester	Gloucester
Workington	Workington	Blackpool or Preston
Worksop	Sheffield	
Worthing	Brighton	
Wrexham	Wrexham	Birkenhead, Chester or Stoke
Yeovil	Yeovil	Bristol or Exeter
York	York	

FORMS

Form	Description
1A	Proposals for an Individual Voluntary Arrangement
1B	Standard conditions to attach to an Individual Voluntary Arrangement
2	Proposals for a Company Voluntary Arrangement

Form 1A   Proposals for an Individual Voluntary Arrangement*

IN THE LEEDS COUNTY COURT   No 6 of 1993

IN BANKRUPTCY

RE: VICTOR LUDO

PROPOSAL FOR A VOLUNTARY ARRANGEMENT WITH CREDITORS PURSUANT TO PART VIII OF THE INSOLVENCY ACT 1986

1   Introduction

1.1   This is the proposal of Victor Ludo of 4 Acacia Road Leeds for the purposes of Part VIII of the Insolvency Act 1986 and the Insolvency Rules 1986 as amended. As appears from the summary of assets and liabilities annexed hereto as Annex A (*not reproduced here*), it is clear that I am insolvent in that I am unable to pay my debts as and when they fall due and my liabilities, including prospective and contingent liabilities, exceed my assets.

1.2   In the circumstances there are two alternatives available to me. I may either petition for my own bankruptcy or seek to enter into a voluntary arrangement with my creditors. For the reasons set out below, I seek a voluntary arrangement which I believe will be acceptable to my creditors.

1.3   I believe that a voluntary arrangement will give rise to a more orderly, quicker and more beneficial realisation of other assets.

1.4   The administrative costs and charges of a voluntary arrangement are likely to be less than in a bankruptcy, as demonstrated in Annex A, and consequently there is likely to be a greater return to unsecured creditors.

---

*Reproduced with the kind permission of Jordans from *Individual Voluntary Arrangements* by Stephen Lawson.

1.5   I will avoid the personal consequences of bankruptcy.

2   Personal history
(Set out here the relevant parts of the debtor's personal history)

3   Assets

Annex A contains full particulars of my assets with an estimate of their respective values. The jointly owned freehold property has been professionally valued by Messrs Nelsons but other assets have not. A copy of the valuation is available for inspection.

3.1   *The house*
It will be seen that there is at present a small margin of equity in the freehold property. It remains to be seen, having regard to the current state of the property market and the level of secured indebtedness, whether there may in fact be a shortfall as regards the secured creditor. If there should be a shortfall upon completion of the sale then this will constitute an unsecured liability for the purpose of dividend. If the property is sold within the next six months then it is likely that there will be a margin of equity, one half of which will be available for purposes of this arrangement. The property is currently being offered for sale by Messrs Nelson at the price of £80,000. The figure shown in Annex A is £72,000 which represents an estimate of what the property is in fact likely to realise. Until sale I anticipate that my wife's earnings will enable her to cover the cost of the mortgage instalments.

3.2   *My car*
My car is subject to a hire purchase agreement and has only a nominal equity. It is in any event proposed that the car should be excluded from assets available for the purposes of voluntary arrangement together with all other assets as defined in section 283(2) of the Insolvency Act 1986.

3.3   *Other assets*
The stock referred to has only a modest value.

3.4   *Cash injection by third party*
My wife will inject £10,000.

4   Debtors

My debtors are shown in Annex A. Whilst it is believed that the figure for debtors is correct and accurate, it will be seen that the individual amounts due are of a comparatively small amount and, in the event of there being difficulty as regards recovery, it is not anticipated that any individual claim will justify the expense of litigation.

5   Liabilities

My unsecured liabilities are set out in Annex A. As regards my boat, it will be seen that this is subject to a leasing agreement in favour of Lomcity Finance and there will be no equity. In the event of the boat being repossessed and sold for a sum less than that shown as being currently due, then Lomcity Finance will be entitled to prove in the voluntary arrangement for their unsecured balance which is estimated at £5,000.

6   Estimated outcome and comparison

There is also shown in Annex A an estimate of the likely outcome of the voluntary arrangement and a comparison with the situation as it is likely to be in bankruptcy. The principal factor in the comparison is the voluntary injection of third party funds, coupled with the saving on professional fees, charges and the Department of Trade and Industry ad valorem duty.

Save as otherwise stated, all figures for assets and liabilities are estimated to the best of my knowledge.

7   Nominee and supervisor

The nominee under the proposal is Mr Kenneth Corkscrew of Corkscrew & Co who is a Chartered Accountant and, so far as I am aware, qualified to act as an insolvency practitioner in relation to this proposal and voluntary arrangement. It is proposed that for the purposes of the Act and Rules, Mr Corkscrew should be the sole supervisor.

If appointed supervisor, Mr Corkscrew will exercise the functions set out in the Act and Rules and as set out in this proposal. He will act as supervisor and not trustee. No assets will vest in Mr Corkscrew. No liability will fall upon him and he will not enter into any contract or other arrangement in a position so as to incur any personal liability.

8   General conditions

8.1   *Secured creditors*
It is not proposed that anything in this proposal should affect the rights of any secured creditor to enforce its security.

8.2 *Preferential creditors*

Any preferential debt will be paid in priority to all unsecured liabilities. Preferential debts will be calculated in accordance with the provisions of the Act and Rules.

8.3 *Voidable transactions*

So far as I am aware, no claim could arise in the event of my bankruptcy under the following provisions of the Act:

section 339 (transactions at an undervalue)
section 340 (preferences)
section 343 (extortionate credit transactions).

8.4 *Guarantees*

No guarantees have been given in respect of any of my liabilities by any other person other than my wife who is jointly liable with me in respect of the secured liabilities charged against our house.

8.5 *Duration*

It is proposed that the voluntary arrangement should last for six months from the date of the creditors' meeting. In that period of time it is anticipated that the Supervisor will have been able to realise all assets, agree all claims and make a final distribution.

8.6 *Proposed dates of distributions*

It is proposed that there will be a single distribution to creditors within the time specified above as soon as all assets have been realised and the liabilities quantified. No specific date can be given because the quantification of liabilities will depend so far as secured creditors are concerned on the realisation of the assets and the calculations of any short fall.

8.7 *Fees to nominee*

The nominee will be entitled to a fee of £1500 plus VAT together with disbursements and all legal costs relating to the application of the interim order and other ancillary legal work.

8.8 *Supervisor's remuneration*

It is proposed that the Supervisor should be remunerated on the basis of work undertaken and time spent. It is estimated that his fees will not exceed £1750 plus VAT. In addition, the Supervisor will be entitled to retain out of the general funds of the arrangement such sums as may be necessary to defray his reasonable expenses and any costs incurred by him by virtue of the employment of any solicitor or other Agent.

8.9 *Guarantees to be offered*

No guarantees are to be offered by any other person and no security is to be given or sought.

8.10   *Funds*
All funds shall be held by the Supervisor who shall open such account as he may consider necessary with a United Kingdom bank in his name as supervisor of the arrangement. The Supervisor will pay into such account all funds received or realised by him under the terms of the arrangement. Any funds held by the Supervisor which, in his opinion, are not required for the immediate purposes of the arrangement may be placed by him on deposit with any recognised bank in the United Kingdom or invested in short dated United Kingdom Government Securities.

8.11   *Continuation of business*
It is not proposed that my business should be continued save for the purpose of realising assets and agreeing liabilities.

8.12   *Further credit facilities*
None are proposed.

8.13   *Functions to be undertaken by the Supervisor*
In his supervisory capacity the Supervisor will oversee my realisation of assets and will directly agree all liabilities. The Supervisor will have complete control of realisations. I will cooperate as fully as possible with him in order that the best possible value may be achieved.

8.14   *Quantification of assets and liabilities*
If any asset is realised for a sum less than that proposed in his proposal and the appendices thereto or if any liabilities shall exceed the estimated figure then that shall not constitute a default within the meaning of section 276 of the Act and shall not entitle any creditor to seek relief from the court either by way of bankruptcy proceedings or otherwise.

8.15   *Conditions*
This proposal should be deemed to incorporate the standard conditions annexed hereto as Annex B (see below).

Victor Ludo
Dated 3rd March 1993

Form 1B Standard Conditions to attach to an Individual Voluntary Arrangement*

ANNEX B
STANDARD CONDITIONS

Interpretation

1.1   These conditions are an integral part of the proposal. Should there be, in any respect, any conflict or ambiguity as between the proposal and these conditions, then the proposal shall prevail.

1.2   'The proposal' means the document annexed hereto and signed by the debtor together with any amendments that may be made thereto, provided that any such amendments shall be in writing signed by the debtor or made pursuant to section 258(2) of the Act.

1.3   Where the arrangement is co-dependent upon the proposal of any other debtor, then these conditions shall apply to all such proposals.

2   In the proposal and these conditions, except where the context otherwise demands:
   (a) 'the Act' means the Insolvency Act 1986;
   (b) 'the Rules' means the Insolvency Rules 1986 and the Insolvency (Amendment) Rules 1987;
   (c) 'the arrangement' means the proposal and these conditions read together.

Approval

3   The approval by creditors of the arrangement pursuant to the Act and the Rules shall be deemed to include approval of and acceptance of these conditions in all respects.

*Reproduced with the kind permission of Jordans from *Individual Voluntary Arrangements* by Stephen Lawson.

Warranty

4   The debtor warrants that he has disclosed to the Nominee full and complete particulars of:
   (a)   all matters without exception relating to his assets and liabilities whether actual or contingent;
   (b)   all matters which are required of him under the Act and the Rules and further warrants that the contents of the proposal are in all respects accurate and true.

Effect of approval (General)

5.1   From the approval of the debtor's proposal pursuant to the provisions of the Act and the Rules:
   (a)   the arrangement shall come into effect;
   (b)   the Supervisor shall exercise the functions given to him by the arrangement and under the Act and Rules.

Duration

5.2   The arrangement shall continue for such period of time as is set out in the proposal provided that such a period of time may be extended by agreement of all parties bound by the proposal in accordance with section 260(2) of the Act. If it is decided to so extend the arrangement, this shall be done by the Supervisor calling a meeting of creditors and in respect of such a meeting the provisions of rules 5.14, 5.15, 5.17 and 5.18(1) shall apply.

Completion

5.3   On completion of the arrangement, the Supervisor shall in writing notify the creditors accordingly.

Default petition

5.4   The Supervisor shall not present any petition pursuant to section 264(1)(c) of the Act unless such has first been agreed upon by a meeting of creditors called pursuant to the provisions of the Rules and these conditions. The debtor shall be given notice of any such meeting and shall be entitled to attend the same.

General power to call meetings

6.1   Rule 6.81 shall apply to the arrangement with the following amendments:
  (a) for 'the official receiver' or 'trustee' read 'the Supervisor';
  (b) for 'the bankruptcy' read 'the debtor';
  (c) for 'the bankrupt' read 'the debtor';
  (d) for 'the statement of affairs' read 'the proposal'.

6.2   If at any meeting so held the Supervisor is dissatisfied with any resolutions so passed, he may apply to the court for directions pursuant to section 263 of the Act and the decision of the court shall be final. There shall be no obligation under the Supervisor to give notice of any such application to any creditor or the debtor unless the court orders otherwise.

Debtor's obligations (to execute deeds etc)

7.1   The debtor shall at the request of the Supervisor execute upon such terms as the Supervisor shall require such deeds, transfers, conveyances, deeds of trust and powers of attorney as may be required by the Supervisor for the implementation of the scheme and the sale of assets and getting in of assets and the protection of the debtor's property included in the proposal provided that the debtor shall not be obliged to execute any power of attorney or deed of trust save in favour of the Supervisor unless otherwise so directed by the court.

Declaration of trust

7.2   The debtor declares that all property comprised in the proposal is held by him on trust for the Supervisor for the purposes of the proposal.

General obligations

7.3   For the general implementation of the arrangement, the debtor shall at the request of the Supervisor, unless the court otherwise directs:
  (a) do all things that the Supervisor shall require;
  (b) institute or defend any legal proceedings which touch or concern the arrangement;
  (c) apply for legal aid for such proceedings;
  (d) attend upon the Supervisor when required;
  (e) deliver to the Supervisor upon receipt any communication received by him (save from the Supervisor) which may touch upon or concern the arrangement.

After-acquired assets

7.4   If prior to the completion of the arrangement the debtor shall become possessed of assets or property (of whatever nature) which are not included in the proposal and the existence of which could not or could not reasonably have been known or envisaged at the date of the creditors' approval of the arrangement, then the debtor shall forthwith disclose the same to the Supervisor and make available to the Supervisor such part of such assets or property as shall allow the Supervisor to pay in full all the liabilities of the debtor with interest at the rate applicable to bankruptcies.

Continuation of business

8.1   The following conditions shall only apply if the debtor's business is to be continued either for:
  (a)   the purpose of eventual sale and the distribution of the sale proceeds to the creditors under the arrangement; or
  (b)   to make funds available for the creditors calculated by reference to the debtor's future income from his business.

8.2   The debtor shall continue his business on his own account and:
  (a)   in his own name; or
  (b)   if applicable, in the name or names in which it was conducted immediately before the date of the interim order.

8.3   Until such time as the arrangement has been completed and the provisions of rule 5.29 complied with, the debtor shall not:
  (a)   enter into any contract or agreement or undertaking for the sale of his business without the consent of the Supervisor;
  (b)   dispose of the goodwill of his business or any assets forming part of or essential to such goodwill without such consent as aforesaid;
  (c)   make any other material changes to the extent, nature or place of his business except:
    (1)   in accordance with any provisions of the arrangement;
    (2)   with the written agreement of the Supervisor;
    (3)   if bound by law to do so.

8.4   Until completion of the arrangement or such time as the debtor ceases to carry on his business, whichever is the earlier, the debtor shall:
  (a)   submit such accounts to the Supervisor as the Supervisor may require;
  (b)   consult the Supervisor as often as the Supervisor may require on the conduct and management of his business and keep the Supervisor informed on any material developments relating thereto.

8.5 For the avoidance of doubt, it is hereby stated that:
  (a) the debtor shall carry on his business as principal and shall be solely responsible for any liabilities incurred therein after the approval of the arrangement;
  (b) notwithstanding the provisions of the arrangement, the creditors shall be at liberty to commence and continue legal proceedings against the debtor in respect of any liabilities incurred by him after the approval of the arrangement.

Taxation

9 The debtor alone shall be responsible for the payment of any taxation liabilities (including any liability for value added tax) arising from the continuation of his business after the approval of the arrangement. Any reference in the proposal to the profits of his buisness means the profits of his business calculated on generally accepted accounting principles before any deduction or provision for tax.

Third parties

10 Where the proposal includes any obligation whatsoever on the part of a third party:
  (a) such third party shall sign the proposal and thereby agree to be bound by the obligation and its due performance;
  (b) such obligation shall be enforceable, at the direction of the Supervisor, by the debtor;
  (c) the failure of such obligation shall be deemed to constitute a failure of the debtor's obligations within the meaning of section 276(1)(a) of the Act and a failure by the debtor to do all such things as may be reasonably required of him within the meaning of section 276(1)(c) of the Act;
  (d) any assets transferred to the Supervisor by any such third party shall be held by the Supervisor on trust for the purposes of the arrangement.

Supervisor's powers

11.1 The powers of the Supervisor shall be those set out in the proposal and these conditions and, subject thereto, the Supervisor shall have all the powers conferred upon an administrative receiver by virtue of Schedule 1 to the Act, provided that the Supervisor shall be under no obligation to exercise such powers unless expressly so required by the arrangement. The powers set out in the said Schedule shall be read and construed as if the same applied to individuals and not bodies corporate.

Paragraphs 8, 15, 16, 19, 21 and 22 of the said Schedule shall not apply.

11.2 The Supervisor may delegate to his firm and any partner, servant, employee or agent of his any or all of his duties hereunder save those which by law he is bound to perform personally.

Application of bankruptcy provisions

12 Unless otherwise provided for in the proposal or the context of the proposal otherwise demands, the following provisions of the Act shall apply to the proposal:

sections 322–326 inclusive;

sections 328, 329 and 330 with such modifications as shall be appropriate to make and render the same relevant to the proposal, provided that unless the proposal so provides no creditor's claim shall carry interest for any period commencing with the day on which the proposal is approved by the creditors' meeting. Creditors' claims shall be calculated as at such date.

Wrongdoing

13 Unless disclosed in the proposal, if, before the completion of the arrangement, the Supervisor becomes aware of any matter which in the context of a bankruptcy would constitute a prior transaction under sections 339, 340 or 343 or a wrongdoing under sections 353 to 362 inclusive, then he shall forthwith report the same to the creditors, convene a creditors' meeting and, subject to the right of the debtor to apply to the court, propose at such meeting the failure of the arrangement.

Completion of the arrangement

14 The term 'completion of the arrangement' shall be defined in accordance with the proposal.

Failure

15.1 The term 'failure of the arrangement' shall mean any of the following events:

(a) any matter which would entitle any person to petition for the bankruptcy of the debtor under sections 264(1)(*c*) and 276 of the Act.

(b) any bankruptcy petition being filed in respect of the debtor in respect of any liability arising after the approval of the arrangement;

(c) the failure of the debtor to comply with any of the terms of the arrangement;

(d) any act or thing which in the opinion of the Supervisor renders the implementation of the arrangement impossible or frustrated unless such act or thing is envisaged or catered for in the proposal, provided that the sale of an asset or realisation of an asset for a sum less than that estimated in the proposal shall not constitute an act or thing within the meaning of this provision unless such is caused by the act or default of the debtor or by someone on his behalf other than the Supervisor;

(e) the failure of any matter set out in the proposal and stated to be a condition precedent of the arrangement;

(f) the passing of a resolution pursuant to condition 13 hereof relating to wrongdoing.

15.2 Where the arrangement has failed within the meaning of condition 15.1 hereof then:

(a) the Supervisor shall report such fact to the creditors and shall issue a certificate of non-compliance pursuant to condition 23 of these conditions;

(b) the Supervisor may call a meeting of creditors pursuant to condition 5.4 hereof;

(c) any creditor bound by the arrangement shall no longer be bound and shall be entitled in respect of his debt to proceed against the debtor as he sees fit.

(d) the Supervisor shall disburse such funds in his hands and in accordance with the provisions of the arrangement unless he is prevented by law from so doing.

15.3 It is hereby declared that the failure of any person, including the debtor, to do any act or thing or to refrain from doing any act or thing within a specified period of time shall not constitute a failure of the scheme unless in the proposal such specified period of time is expressed to be of the essence. Any condition precedent shall be 'of the essence' unless otherwise provided for in the proposal.

Directions

16 If the Supervisor is for whatever reason uncertain as to what action he should take in any situation, he shall within his own discretion:

(a) seek the advice of the creditors' committee (if any);

(b) seek the advice of the creditors;

(c) apply so far as is possible the Act and Rules as they relate to bankruptcy and, subject thereto;

(d) apply to the court for directions.

Expenditure on assets

17 The Supervisor shall only spend any funds in his hands for the purposes of repairing, completing or altering any asset held by him or by the debtor on trust for the purposes of the arrangement if:

(a) he is of the opinion that, as a result, the asset or assets concerned are likely to become more readily saleable or increase in value by an amount greater than that of the expenditure thus incurred;

(b) if so bound to do so by the terms of the proposal.

Agreement of claims

18.1 As soon as possible after the approval of the debtor's proposal (provided no application under section 262 is pending), the Supervisor shall send a notice to each person shown in the debtor's proposal or statement of affairs as a creditor requiring him/her or it to provide such details as the Supervisor thinks fit of the amount claimed to be due from the debtor.

18.2 The Supervisor shall:

(a) send a similar notice to any other person to whom he believes the debtor may be indebted;

(b) be entitled but not obligated to insert a similar notice in such newspapers as he considers appropriate;

(c) be entitled to ask for any further details or documentation he thinks necessary for the purpose of establishing the amount due to any person claiming to be a creditor.

18.3 No creditor shall be entitled to receive any payment or dividend from the Supervisor or any other person under the terms of the arrangement unless:

(a) he is bound by the arrangement by virtue of section 260 or by an undertaking to that effect; or

(b) the Supervisor has admitted his claim for the purpose of participation in any payment or dividend under the arrangement, provided that the Supervisor may, if he thinks fit, admit the claim of any other person to whom the debtor appears to be indebted as at the date of the creditors' meeting save that, if the aggregate of such indebtedness exceeds £1,000, then prior to admission the Supervisor shall notify all creditors bound. No such further claim shall be so admitted unless the creditor undertakes to be bound by the arrangement.

18.4   Unless otherwise agreed by the creditors in general meeting or otherwise provided for in the proposal, no creditor shall be entitled to participate in the arrangement unless that creditor's debt is one provable in bankruptcy within the meaning of the Act and Rules.

Priority of payments

19   The funds held by the Supervisor shall be applied strictly in accordance with the terms of the proposal but, subject thereto, in the order of priority as would apply in bankruptcy.

Payments to creditors

20.1   The Supervisor shall not make any payment to creditors until at least 28 days have elapsed since the date of the creditors' meeting approving the arrangement. Subject thereto and provided no application under section 262 or 263(3) is pending, he shall make payments or distribution to creditors:
 (a)   at the time or times specified in the arrangement;
 (b)   if no other provision is made, at such time or times as he considers appropriate.

20.2   If any dividends remain unclaimed on completion of the arrangement, then:
 (a)   the Supervisor shall pay the amounts thereof by way of dividend amongst the remaining creditors;
 (b)   the Supervisor shall have no further duties, obligations or liabilities to those creditors not claiming a dividend.

20.3   Section 325(1) of the Act shall apply for the purpose of the arrangement.

Bank account costs and expenses

21.1   The Supervisor shall open one or more accounts with a United Kingdom branch or branches of a recognised bank in his name as Supervisor of the arrangement and pay into such account or accounts all the funds received or realised by him under the terms of the arrangement. Any funds held by the Supervisor which in his opinion are not required for the immediate purposes of the arrangement may be placed by him on deposit with any recognised bank in the United Kingdom or invested in short dated United Kingdom Government Securities.

21.2   The Supervisor shall be authorised to pay from funds under his control:
   (a)   the fees and disbursements set out in the proposal;
   (b)   any expenses properly incurred by him in pursuance of the arrangement including, without prejudice to the generality of the foregoing:
      (1)   the fees of any solicitors appointed to assist the debtor or the nominee in connection with the application of the interim order and proceedings related thereto, if any;
      (2)   the fees of any valuer or agent retained by the Supervisor to value or dispose of any of the assets assigned to the Supervisor or held by the debtor on trust for the purpose of the arrangement pursuant to condition 7.2 above;
      (3)   unless the court orders otherwise, the cost of any action to which the Supervisor is a party wherein costs are incurred by him or awarded against him in his capacity as Supervisor;
      (4)   any tax assessable on the Supervisor in his capacity as such;
      (5)   the costs of complying with any obligation laid upon the Supervisor by virtue of the arrangement, the Act, the Rules or any other rules, regulations or orders made thereunder;
      (6)   such other sums as he shall be authorised or required to pay by virtue of the arrangement or any rule of law.

21.3   There shall be paid to the nominee, whether or not he is the Supervisor, such fees and disbursements as are specified in the arrangement.

21.4   Subject to any contrary provision in the arrangement, the amount to be paid to the Supervisor for his services shall be:
   (a)   as provided for in the proposal and subject thereto;
   (b)   determined by the creditors' committee;
   (c)   if no committee is established or the committee does not determine the amount, then as determined by the creditors in general meeting;
   (d)   if not determined by the committee or the creditors, then calculated according to the scale applicable to the Official Receiver when he is acting as trustee in bankruptcy.
If he is dissatisfied by the amount determined as above, the Supervisor, the debtor or any creditor may apply for the amount to be determined by the court, but any such application must be made within 28 days of the applicant becoming aware of the amount.

21.5   The Supervisor may draw sums on account of his fees and disbursements from time to time as he thinks fit.

Health of debtor

22   Should the debtor die before the completion of the arrangement, the arrangement shall be binding on his personal representatives.

Termination

23.1   The arrangement shall cease to have effect once:
(a)   there are no further funds or assets held by the Supervisor or the debtor on trust for the purposes of the arrangement; or
(b)   the Supervisor has issued a certificate of due completion or a certificate of non-compliance.

23.2   The issue of a certificate of non-compliance shall:
(a)   not release the debtor from any obligation placed upon him under the arrangement;
(b)   not prejudice the Supervisor's rights to exercise any of the powers given to him under the arrangement, including the power to realise any of the assets under his control and to distribute any funds in his hands in accordance with the terms of the arrangement.

23.3   When he issues a certificate of due completion or a certificate of non-compliance, the Supervisor shall forthwith give notice of that fact to the debtor and all known creditors.

Vacancy in office

24.1   Should a vacancy arise in the office of Supervisor by death or otherwise, that vacancy may be filled by the creditors at a meeting:
(a)   convened for the purpose by:
(1)   any creditor;
(2)   any person acting as a representative of any member of the creditors' committee (if any);
(3)   any person who is in partnership with the Supervisor immediately before the vacancy occurred;
(b)   and chaired by:
(1)   the convenor;
(2)   any person qualified to act as an insolvency practitioner in relation to the debtor;
(3)   a partner or senior employee of the former Supervisor's firm experienced in insolvency matters.

Ambiguity

25   Where any part of these conditions incorporates any provisions of the Act or Rules and such incorporation gives rise to an ambiguity or inconsistency, then the Supervisor shall within his own absolute discretion resolve such ambiguity or inconsistency as he shall think fit and the exercise of such discretion shall not be open to any challenge by legal proceedings or otherwise by any creditor bound by the arrangement or by the debtor or by any person on their or his behalf.

Amendment

26   No amendment or variation of the terms of the arrangement shall be permitted after the approval of the arrangement unless so agreed at a general meeting of creditors called pursuant to condition 6 hereof and, at such meeting, rule 5.18(1) shall apply. No amendment or variation shall be made without the consent in writing of the debtor and any third party affected thereby.

FORM 2   Proposals for a Company Voluntary Arrangement

IN THE MATTER OF LOOKWELL CONTACTS LIMITED   No   of 1993

AND IN THE MATTER OF THE INSOLVENCY ACT 1986

We, Richard Nixon of 174 Baker Street London and Norman Bush of 5 Acacia Gardens London propose a voluntary arrangement or composition in satisfaction of the debts of Lookwell Contacts Ltd (hereinafter called 'the Company'). Our proposals are as follows:

1   The Company operated as opthalmic opticians. It traded from premises at 2 Oxford Street, London W1. The registered office of the company is at 23 Baker Street, London W1. The Company was incorporated on the 15th June 1990 with registered number 123456 and has traded at Oxford Street since its incorporation. The Company purchased a business of opthalmic opticians in 1990 for a total of £70,000. A purchaser was found for the business and in January 1993 the business, its goodwill and lease were sold to an independent third party for £140,000 (part of the consideration being payable by instalments). It was believed that the proceeds of the sale would be sufficient to pay all creditors in full. The books of the Company, however, had not been written up since November 1992 because of the serious ill-health of the book-keeper and when the true position was discovered on 20th February 1992 professional advice was immediately sought and no further payments to creditors were made.

2   We feel that a voluntary arrangement would be of benefit to the creditors of the Company because dividend prospects would be enhanced by virtue of the savings in costs and lesser liabilities as reflected in the comparative figures which are attached to the Statement of Affairs which forms Annex 1 (*not reproduced here*) to these proposals ('the Statement of Affairs').

3   The assets of the Company and their respective values are set out on the Statement of Affairs.

4   The assets of the Company are not charged to any creditor.

5   All the assets of the Company are proposed to be included in the voluntary arrangement.

6   No other property, other than the assets of the Company itself is proposed to be included in the voluntary arrangement.

7   So far as is within our immediate knowledge, the nature and amounts of the Company's liabilities together with the manner in which they are proposed to be met, modified, postponed or otherwise dealt with are as follows:
   (a) Lloyds Bank are owed £52,000 approximately which is personally guaranteed by ourselves. The proposed distribution to the bank is reflected in paragraph 13 of our proposal.
   (b) Preferential creditors amount to £15,500. These will be paid in accordance with the provisions of paragraph 13 of our proposals.

8   There are no persons who are connected with the Company who are creditors except Columbus Travel Ltd and Sight Unseen Ltd whose debts are shown separately on the Statement of Affairs. In the event of the Supervisor establishing that such creditors do exist, their claims will be subordinated to those of all other classes of creditors. They will not rank for dividend purposes until all classes of creditors are paid in full and the costs and expenses of the voluntary arrangement have been fully discharged but they reserve their rights to vote on these proposals.

9   To the best of our knowledge there are no circumstances giving rise to the possibility of claims in respect of transactions at an undervalue, preferences extortionate credit transactions or circumstances which would give rise to the invalidity of floating charges except that a payment of £42,092 was paid to the Company's bank on 10 January 1993 and £7,032 in February 1993 prior to the time when we discovered that the proceeds of the sale of the Company's business were insufficient to meet all its liabilities in full.

10   It is proposed that the various class of creditors will be paid as hereinafter appears.

11   Distraint has not been levied on any chattel assets belonging to the Company. One creditor whose claim is in dispute has issued proceedings.

12   The proposed duration of the voluntary arrangement is three years. The Supervisor will have absolute discretion to extend the duration as he feels fit.

13   Distributions to the various classes of creditors will be made as follows:
   (a) *Preferential creditors*
        Preferential creditors will be paid in full within six months of the

voluntary arrangement being approved by creditors or within one
month of their claims being agreed, which ever is the later. It is
proposed that all outstanding returns will be submitted to Inland
Revenue and Customs and Excise within three months of the
agreement of the voluntary arrangement.

(b) *Unsecured creditors*

It is proposed that unsecured creditors receive in full settlement
of their claims against the Company the assets available to the
Company after the payment of the claims of the preferential creditors
and the costs, the first dividends to be paid within three months
of the preferential creditors being paid off and in any event not
later than nine months after approval of these proposals and thereafter
every three months.

Columbus Travel Ltd and Sight Unseen Ltd have agreed to defer
their claims provided that these proposals are approved by creditors.

14   We propose that the Company will pay to the Nominee a sum of £2,000
plus VAT together with all disbursements and legal costs.

15   We propose that the Supervisor be remunerated and his expenses paid
out of the assets of the Company in accordance with the time spent by him
according to his time charges and expenses as and when incurred with a
maximum of £5,500 (to include the finalisation of the accounts and agreement
of tax liabilities).

16   We do not propose that there should be any guarantees from ourselves
or other persons as to the distributions to creditors referred to.

17   The Supervisor will open a bank account at a major UK clearing bank
for the purpose of receiving funds from the Company in order to discharge
the liabilities to the preferential and unsecured creditors. This account will
be under the exclusive control of the Supervisor.

18   We propose that the functions to be undertaken by the Supervisor shall
include the duties referred to in the paragraphs above and in addition an
obligation to monitor the implementation of the proposals on a regular basis.

19   The Supervisor will be responsible for payments to all creditors of the
Company and the agreement of their claims. In the event that the Supervisor
is in a position to pay a dividend but has not yet received claims from a
creditor he shall send to that creditor by recorded delivery to its registered
office in the case of a company and to its normal trading address in any
other case, a letter advising them that unless such a claim is received at the
Supervisor's office within 14 days of delivery of the letter, the distribution
will be made excluding the creditor and no further claims will be entertained.

20 For the avoidance of doubt, it is proposed that nothing under the terms of this voluntary arrangement shall be interpreted as imposing any personal liability upon the Supervisor, his firm or his staff in any way whatsoever.

21 The Supervisor shall be empowered to instruct such agents and solicitors as he considers fit in his absolute discretion for the purposes of carrying out the purposes of this voluntary arrangement and in particular in relation to the collection of outstanding monies for the purchaser.

22 If the Supervisor, in his absolute discretion considers that the company voluntary arrangement has failed, he shall write to creditors advising them of this fact whereupon he will present a petition for the compulsory winding up of the Company. If any creditor wishes to convene a meeting of creditors to consider this decision they shall, within seven days from the date of the letter sent by the Supervisor in this regard, inform the Supervisor of his desire to convene a meeting of creditors and shall lodge with the Supervisor the sum of £500 to cover the costs of convening such a meeting.

23 Kenneth Corkscrew of Corkscrew & Co, 77 Sunset Avenue, London being a Fellow of the Institute of Chartered Accountants of England and Wales is proposed as Supervisor. He holds an insolvency licence issued by the said institute and is qualified to act as an insolvency practitioner.

Directors

Dated the 1st day of March 1993